SECOND EDITION

2

STANDARD GRADE

Home Economics

course notes

× Alastair MacGregor ×

Text © 2007 Alastair MacGregor
Design and layout © 2007 Leckie & Leckie
Cover photo © Stockbyte / Getty images
Cover design by Caleb Rutherford

01/06072007

ISBN 978-1-84372-493-3

Published by
Leckie & Leckie Ltd, 3rd Floor, 4 Queen Street, Edinburgh EH2 1JE
Phone: 0131 220 6831   Fax: 0131 225 9987
enquiries@leckieandleckie.co.uk   www.leckieandleckie.co.uk

Special thanks to
Project One Publishing Solutions, Edinburgh (Project management and editing)
The Partnership Publishing Solutions (Design and page layout)
Ellustration (illustrations)

Printed in the UK by Nuffield Press

A CIP Catalogue record for this book is available from the British Library.

® Leckie & Leckie is a registered trademark.
Leckie & Leckie is a division of Huveaux plc

Acknowledgements
Leckie & Leckie has made every effort to trace all copyright holders.
If any have been inadvertently overlooked, we will be pleased to make the necessary arrangements.
We would like to thank the following for permission to reproduce their material:
Waste Watch for a pie chart taken from their website: www.wasteonline.org.uk (p. 83).
Leckie & Leckie would like to thank the following for permission to reproduce their copyright material without charge:
David Beardsley for an image taken from http://reducetheuse.co.uk (pp. 79 & 80); The Energy Saving Trust for use of the Energy Saving Trust 'Recommended' logo (p. 80); The Fairtrade Foundation for use of their logo (p. 104); The Vegetarian Society for use of their logo (p.104); The Vegan Society for use of their logo (p. 104); The Soil Association for the Organic Standard logo (p. 104); The British Union for the Abolition of Vivisection (BUAV) for use of the 'BUAV Approved' logo (p.105); The British Toy & Hobby Association for the Lion Mark logo (p. 107); Kitemark reproduced with the permission of BSI under licence number 2002SK/0113 (p. 107); The British Electrotechnical Approvals Board for the BEAB Approved logo (p. 107); The Council for Registered Gas Installers for the CORGI logo (p. 107); The British Board of Film Classification for use of their film classification logos (p. 108); APACS for use of the 'Chip and Pin' logo (p. 119); IMRG for use of the 'Internet Shopping Is Safe' logo (p. 123).

..

CONTENTS

INTRODUCTION

Welcome to *Standard Grade Home Economics Course Notes*. This book will help you as you progress your way through your Standard Grade Home Economics Course.

The main chapters of the book are arranged to cover the main areas of essential knowledge for the course:

- Eating a variety of foods contributes to health
- Current dietary advice
- Individuals have varying dietary needs
- Cleanliness is important in relation to health
- Safe working practices
- Design features
- Physical needs of individuals and families
- Management of expenditure.

This revised book provides the most up-to-date information relating to the study of Standard Grade Home Economics. The **Course Notes** now include activities linked to each of the chapters which will help with revision and test your knowledge and understanding of the key facts and concepts. A new feature called 'Big Picture' has been added to provide new information about topical matters. You will not be asssessed on these areas in your exam, but you should find them interesting and informative.

Course assessment

Standard Grade Home Economics contains three main elements which are assessed:

- Knowledge and Understanding (KU)
- Handling Information (HI)
- Practical and Organisational Skills (POS).

Standard Grade Home Economics is available at three different levels:

- Foundation level
- General level
- Credit level.

You will be assessed in your KU and HI by completing an examination paper.

- The Foundation exam lasts for 1 hour.
- The General exam lasts for 1 hour.
- The Credit exam lasts for 1 hour and 15 minutes.

The maximum number of marks allocated to each examination paper is:

● the Foundation paper is worth 60 marks
● the General paper is worth 70 marks
● the Credit paper is worth 80 marks.

KU is assessed by questions in the examination paper. This book covers all the KU knowledge that you will require for the course and the exam. If you have a good knowledge and understanding of all the content in this book, you should do well in the KU exam questions.

HI is assessed by questions in the examination paper. These questions take the format of a given case study with a chart of information. You will be asked to consider the case study, interpret the chart, and to make choices for a particular situation. You will need to provide explanations for your choices.

You can practise both KU and HI type questions using Leckie and Leckie's *Questions in Standard Grade Home Economics* book.

You will not have a formal exam for **POS** but you will be assessed in class by your teacher. This will involve you planning and carrying out practical exercises and completing a practical assignment.

How to use this book

Information that is useful to all pupils but is assessed only at **Credit** level is indicated by this graphic:

Information that is generally useful or interesting but will not be assessed is indicated by this graphic:

Hints and tips that are particularly useful for assessment purposes (avoiding common errors, things to look out for, etc.) are indicated by this graphic:

Throughout the chapters there are **activities** which require pupils to remember and/or apply some of the information they have just learnt. These activities are indicated by this graphic:

Some activities direct pupils to **websites** to follow-up some information, and these are indicated by this graphic:

Links to these websites can be found at: **www.leckieandleckie.co.uk** by clicking on the Learning Lab button and navigating to the Standard Grade Home Economics Course Notes page.

Important technical terminology is highlighted in the text, and **definitions** given in the Word Bank feature, indicated by this graphic:

A **Quick Quiz** is given at the end of each chapter, giving pupils an opportunity to see if they've remembered the key points in the chapter.

Answers to the activities and the end-of chapter quizzes are on pages 126–128.

CHAPTER 1: Eating a variety of foods contributes to good health

In this chapter

- The main nutrients, their sources and functions
- Relationship between water, non-starch polysaccharides and health
- Health and nutrient intake
- Interrelationship of nutrients

THE MAIN NUTRIENTS, THEIR SOURCES AND FUNCTIONS

There will always be questions in the exam paper about **nutrients**. The charts on pages 7–12 detail all the information that you will need to know in the examination. Some information is required only by candidates who will sit a Credit examination.

NUTRIENT	FOOD SOURCES	FUNCTIONS IN THE BODY
Protein	Animal sources: meat, fish, milk, cheese and eggs. Vegetable sources: peas, beans, nuts, lentils and cereals.	Required for the growth, repair and maintenance of body tissues. Any excess protein can be broken down and used as a source of energy.
	Protein is made up of amino acids. There are over 20 different amino acids. Adults require eight of these amino acids for growth, repair and maintenance of body tissue and cells. Children require ten. Animal sources contain all essential amino acids and are called **High Biological Value** (HBV) proteins. Plant sources do not contain all the essential amino acids and are called **Low Biological Value** (LBV) proteins. Soya bean is a vegetable source of protein but contains all ten essential amino acids.	

Nutrition: the study of food and how the body uses it.
Nutrients: chemicals that are found in food. The body needs nutrients if it is to work properly.

NUTRIENT	FOOD SOURCES	FUNCTIONS IN THE BODY
Carbohydrate – sugar and starch	Cereals and cereal foods, vegetables, fruits, milk, refined sugar and products containing refined sugar (e.g. cakes and biscuits, jams, soft drinks).	A major source of energy. Excess carbohydrate that is not used for energy will be converted into body fat and so can provide warmth.

Carbohydrates can be subdivided into three main groups:

- **Monosaccharides**: *glucose* (naturally found in fruit and plant juices), *fructose* (naturally found in some fruits and vegetables, as well as honey), and *galactose* (produced as a result of the digestive process).
- **Disaccharides**: *sucrose* (naturally found in sugar cane and beet and in some vegetables, e.g. carrots); *maltose* (formed during digestion and in the fermentation of grain); *lactose* (found only in milk).
- **Polysaccharides**: *starch* is a polysaccharide found in bread, flour, potatoes and cakes. *Non-starch polysaccharides* (NSP) are a form of polysaccharide. See pages 13–14 for more information on NSP.

NUTRIENT	FOOD SOURCES	FUNCTIONS IN THE BODY
Fat	Animal sources: butter, lard, cream, meat, oily fish, milk, cheese and many baked foods. Vegetable sources: olive oil, margarine, nuts and some salad dressings.	A concentrated source of energy for the body. Warmth – excess fat is stored under the skin, providing an insulating layer. Provides essential fatty acids such as omega 3. Provides an adequate source of fat-soluble vitamins A, D, E and K.

Fats can be classified as either **saturated** or **unsaturated**. Saturated fats are mainly from animal sources and are considered to be bad for health. Unsaturated fats are considered to be better for the body. Unsaturated fats can be further divided into **monounsaturated fats** (e.g. olive oil and fish oils) and **polyunsaturated fats** (e.g. polyunsaturated margarine). Essential fatty acids are found in vegetable oils and must be obtained directly from foods as the body cannot manufacture them. This is one reason why we are advised to consume unsaturated rather than saturated fats.

Vitamins

Vitamins are essential to general health. Each vitamin is required in only relatively small quantities and each has a particular function in the body. Vitamins are classified according to whether they are **soluble in fat or in water**.

Fortified: to have nutrients, for example vitamins or minerals, added to a food product.
Small intestine: a part of the digestive system.
Invalid: a person who is ill, usually for a long time, and requires care by another person.
Housebound: unable to leave the house, usually because they are elderly, infirm or disabled.

Fat-soluble vitamins

NUTRIENT	FOOD SOURCES	FUNCTIONS IN THE BODY
Vitamin A – found in food as either retinol in animal sources or as carotene in plant sources. Anti-oxidant	Animal sources: liver, butter, cheese, margarine, sardines, meat, eggs, cheese and fish liver oils. Plant sources: spinach, carrots and green vegetables and mango.	Classed as an antioxidant vitamin, it protects against various types of cancer. Required for growth in children. Assists with good vision – particularly vision in dim light. Protects surface tissues (e.g. linings of the nose, mouth, throat and eyes)
Carotene is converted into vitamin A in the **small intestine**. Six units of carotene are equal to one unit of retinol.		

NUTRIENT	FOOD SOURCES	FUNCTIONS IN THE BODY
Vitamin D	The main source of vitamin D is the action of sunlight on the skin. Food sources include: fish liver oils, oily fish, egg yolk, liver, margarine, **fortified** breakfast cereals.	Essential with calcium and phosphorus for the development of strong bones and teeth. Promotes quicker healing of bone fractures. Allows calcium to be absorbed in the small intestine. Required for blood clotting.
The action of sunlight on the skin results in the formation of vitamin D in the body. People who do not get out into the sunshine (e.g. the **housebound** and **invalids**) may suffer from a deficiency.		

CREDIT

NUTRIENT	FOOD SOURCES	FUNCTIONS IN THE BODY
Vitamin E Anti-oxidant	Vegetable oils, eggs, liver, meat, wheat germ, oatmeal, margarine. Leafy green vegetables contain a small amount.	Classed as an antioxidant vitamin as it is thought to be linked to the prevention of heart disease. Involved in the maintenance of cell membranes.

NUTRIENT	FOOD SOURCES	FUNCTIONS IN THE BODY
Vitamin K	Leafy green vegetables such as broccoli and spinach, eggs, milk, yoghurt.	Required for the clotting of blood, particularly after an injury. (New-born babies are given vitamin K at birth either by injection or by mouth.)

Water-soluble vitamins

NUTRIENT	FOOD SOURCES	FUNCTIONS IN THE BODY
Vitamin C Anti-oxidant	Mainly in fruits and vegetables: peppers, blackcurrants, cabbage, strawberries, citrus fruit, green vegetables, potatoes.	Classed as an antioxidant vitamin, protecting molecules in the body from damage by free radicals. Helps in the formation of connective tissue. Helps in the absorption of iron. Helps prevent infections. Essential in the formation of the walls of blood vessels.
Vitamin B1 – Thiamin	Wheat germ, oatmeal, whole wheat, bran, whole brown rice, yeast, Marmite, green leafy vegetables, meat – especially bacon, ham and pork.	Release of energy from carbohydrates. Growth and functioning of nervous system. Maintains muscle tone. Note: alcohol prevents the absorption of this vitamin.
Vitamin B2 – Riboflavin	Milk, eggs, green vegetables, yeast, liver, kidney, meat. Some vitamin B is manufactured in the intestines.	Release of energy from protein, carbohydrates and fat. Required for normal growth in children. Required for the repair of nails, skin and hair.
Folic acid	Liver, kidneys, dark leafy vegetables, whole grain cereals, whole-wheat bread, pulses.	Required in the formation of red blood cells. Has a role in the prevention of neural tube defects (e.g. spina bifida) in developing fetuses.

> *Antioxidant vitamins*
>
> **Vitamins A**, **C** and **E** are sometimes referred to as **antioxidant vitamins**. Research indicates that sufficient intake of vitamin C offers vital protection against cancer. Studies also indicate that higher levels of vitamins A, C and E reduce the risk of heart disease.

Minerals

Like vitamins, minerals are essential to general health. Each one is required in only relatively small quantities, but each has particular functions in the body.

NUTRIENT	FOOD SOURCES	FUNCTIONS IN THE BODY
Iron	Red meat – particularly offal (kidneys, liver), bread, flour, cereal products, green leafy vegetables.	Required for red blood cell formation. Red blood cells assist in the movement of oxygen around the body.
Iron is required for the formation of a substance in the blood called **haemoglobin**. This is the substance that red blood cells use to transport oxygen from the lungs to body tissues.		

NUTRIENT	FOOD SOURCES	FUNCTIONS IN THE BODY
Calcium	Milk, cheese, yoghurt, flour, bread, green vegetables, canned fish, soy beans.	Growth and development of bones and teeth. Required for the normal clotting of blood. Required for the normal functioning of nerves and muscles.
The material that gives teeth and bones their hardness is **calcium phosphate**, which is made from the minerals calcium and phosphorus. Although both are required for strong bones and teeth, they also have important independent functions in the body.		

NUTRIENT	FOOD SOURCES	FUNCTIONS IN THE BODY
Fluoride	Often found dissolved in drinking water if the water supply has been fluoridated. Also found in small quantities in tea and saltwater fish.	Essential for hardening the enamel of teeth. Ensures that bones have the correct amounts of minerals deposited in them.
Fluoride is often found in commercial toothpastes. Excessive fluoride in the diet can lead to the **discolouration** or **mottling** of teeth.		

NUTRIENT	FOOD SOURCES	FUNCTIONS IN THE BODY
Sodium	Salt, bacon, cheese, some savoury snacks products, e.g. crisps.	Required to maintain the correct concentration of body fluids in the body. Required for correct muscle activity. Required for correct nerve activity.

NUTRIENT	FOOD SOURCES	FUNCTIONS IN THE BODY
Phosphorus	Found in most foods, especially milk, milk products, cereal products, meat and meat products, nuts.	Works in conjunction with calcium to give strength to bones and teeth. Phosphorus is a component of all cells and is required so that the body can obtain energy from foods.
Most foods rich in calcium are also rich in phosphorus, but not vice versa.		

For you to do

1 List the main nutrients that would be found in the following snack: glass of milk, baked potato with cheese, apple.
2 **a** Which nutrients play a role in the body relating to energy?
  b Which nutrients play a role in the body relating to healthy blood?
3 Copy and complete the following flowchart which illustrates the main groupings of carbohydrates.

HINTS & TIPS

Generally, all examination papers will ask a question about the sources and functions of at least one of the major nutrients listed above. You would not normally be asked to give more than two functions of a particular nutrient. It is important that you know the main food sources of a nutrient, because a question might ask you to identify nutrients found in a specific meal or food.

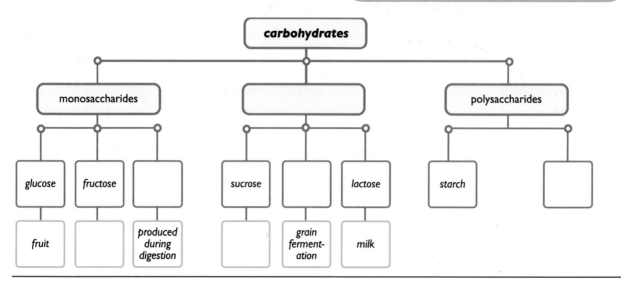

RELATIONSHIP BETWEEN WATER, NON-STARCH POLYSACCHARIDES AND HEALTH

All of the nutrients mentioned are important for a healthy body. To work effectively and efficiently, the body also requires water and non-starch polysaccharides.

Water

Water is not a nutrient but it is essential for life. The human body is about 65% water.

FOOD SOURCES	FUNCTIONS IN THE BODY
Most foods contain water. Fruits and vegetables consist mainly of water. Water is supplied in the diet as drinking water as well as in liquid products such as milk.	Required for all body fluids (e.g. blood, saliva, sweat, urine). Helps in the removal of waste products from body tissues and organs. Some nutrients are dissolved in water for better absorption. Lubricates joints and **mucous membranes**.

WORD BANK

Mucous membranes: thin membranes protecting the surfaces of, for example, the nose and mouth; these need to remain moist.

Dehydration: excessive loss of water in the body.

Lactation: breastfeeding.

Water should be consumed daily. During exercise and in hot weather we sweat. This means that our body loses water that needs to be replaced. Sweating cools the body as perspiration **evaporates** from the surface of the skin. Water is lost daily through sweat, urine, faeces and breathing, and so needs to be replaced.

Extra water may be required during illness, when a raised temperature may increase sweating or when vomiting or diarrhoea has occurred (both of which can cause rapid **dehydration**, especially in small children). Additional water is needed during **lactation** when milk is being produced to breastfeed babies.

Non-starch polysaccharide

Non-starch polysaccharide (NSP) provides the firm and fibrous structure of fruits, vegetables and cereal products. This part of the food is the part that cannot be digested by the body. For this reason, NSP is not classed as a nutrient.

HINTS & TIPS

NSP is some times also referred to as fibre, dietary fibre or roughage. Use any of these terms (except roughage) when answering examination questions.

Faeces: the solid waste removed from the body through the bowels.

Cholesterol: a soft, waxy substance found among the fats in the bloodstream and in all your body's cells (see page 26).

Diverticular disease: a disease affecting the small intestine (see page 25).

FOOD SOURCES	FUNCTIONS IN THE BODY
Wholegrain cereals (e.g. oats, wheat, rice, wholemeal bread). Fruits (especially in the skins) and vegetables, especially potato skins and leafy vegetables.	NSP absorbs water and binds other food residues to itself, so making the **faeces** soft and bulky and easy to remove from the body. NSP helps to 'mop up' any poisonous toxins found in waste products. NSP gives a feeling of fullness and so may be useful as part of a calorie-controlled diet. This is due to the fact that a diet rich in NSP will slow down the digestive process and so we feel 'fuller' for a longer period of time. Consumption of NSP has been associated with reductions in **cholesterol**. A diet rich in NSP can prevent constipation, bowel diseases (such as cancer of the colon) and **diverticular disease**.

HEALTH AND NUTRIENT INTAKE

The following terms are often used when talking about nutrition:

- **balanced diet**: a diet in which the correct amounts of nutrients are available for a person's needs
- **under-nutrition**: an insufficient total intake of nutrients to allow the body to function correctly
- **malnutrition**: an unbalanced or incorrect intake of nutrients
- **metabolism**: a series of chemical reactions that takes place within the body and enables the body to function correctly.

The relationship between health and energy

Energy is not a nutrient. When your body digests nutrients (fat, carbohydrate and protein), energy is released, allowing your body to carry out all its functions and activities. It is important that the amount of energy supplied by your food equals the amount of energy you require for your body to carry out all its functions and activities.

- If you do not consume enough energy-providing foods, you may become tired and listless – you are 'lacking in energy'. The body must have energy so if you are not consuming sufficient energy-rich foods, your body may use protein as its source of energy. This means that you may become deficient in protein.
- If you take in too much energy from the food you eat and your body does not use it all, it is stored as fat.

It is important that you get this energy balance right.

In your written examination you may be asked to identify the nutrients found in specific foods. This is why it is important that you have a good knowledge of nutrition.

The relationship between health and protein

Protein is essential to life. But what happens when the protein balance is not right? If you take in too much protein, the excess is converted to fat and stored in your body. This can cause you to become overweight. However, if you do not consume enough protein-rich foods, your body cannot carry out its normal functions of growth and repair. On page 7 we looked at HBV and LBV protein foods. HBV protein foods contain all eight essential amino acids required for growth and repair in adults. LBV protein foods are missing at least one of these essential amino acids. These foods can compensate for each other's deficiencies if eaten together and in sufficient quantities. A good example is beans and wholemeal toast. The amino acids that are missing in beans are found in the toast and vice versa, that is, one food **complements** the other.

In many developing countries the traditional diet is based on cereals such as rice. The protein content of cereal products is generally of a low biological value, so the diets of people in these areas may be deficient in protein. By contrast, in developed countries there is generally an excess of protein in the diet, leading to storage of fat in the body.

The multi-nutrient value of food

Most foods contain more than one nutrient, and so are of use to the body in different ways. It is important that a balanced diet is eaten to ensure that a good balance of nutrients is consumed, as no single food provides the body with all the nutrients that it requires to function properly. Some foods, such as sugar, contain only one nutrient (in this case carbohydrate) and so are of more limited use to the body.

INTERRELATIONSHIP OF NUTRIENTS

Your body requires a large number of nutrients if it is to function well. Many nutrients have similar functions, and some nutrients work together for specific functions.

Calcium, phosphorus and vitamin D

Calcium, phosphorus and vitamin D have some separate functions in the body, but they also have an important role to play together.

The material which gives both bones and teeth their hardness is a substance called **calcium phosphate**. The process is called **calcification**, where bones and teeth become **enmeshed** with calcium phosphate and become stronger. A supply of both calcium and phosphorus is required before this process can take place.

The amount of calcium that is available to the body is controlled by vitamin D. If there is insufficient vitamin D in the diet, less calcium will be available.

Iron and vitamin C

Iron and vitamin C have an important role to play together, as well as having separate functions in the body.

Vitamin C plays an important role in assisting with the absorption of iron. The body can readily absorb only about 10% of the iron that is present in food. The remainder must be changed into a form of iron that the body can easily absorb. Vitamin C helps in this process. For this reason it is important when planning meals to ensure that there are sufficient foods rich in vitamin C.

Complement: to complete something, make up a whole. (Do not confuse with *compliment*.)

Factors affecting the absorption of nutrients

There are a variety of factors that assist in the absorption of nutrients and a variety of factors that hinder the absorption of nutrients.

Calcium and iron

The diagram below shows the factors that help the body to absorb calcium and iron, and the factors that make it harder for the body to absorb calcium and iron.

The Credit level examination paper may have a question about the interrelationships between different nutrients. When answering this type of question it is important that you do not just restate the function of each individual nutrient – this is not what the question is asking. You need to explain how the nutrients work together.

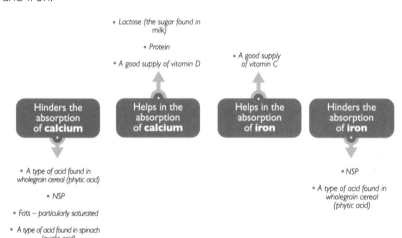

* Lactose (the sugar found in milk)

* Protein

* A good supply of vitamin D

* A good supply of vitamin C

| Hinders the absorption of **calcium** | Helps in the absorption of **calcium** | Helps in the absorption of **iron** | Hinders the absorption of **iron** |

* A type of acid found in wholegrain cereal (phytic acid)

* NSP

* Fats – particularly saturated

* A type of acid found in spinach (oxalic acid)

* NSP

* A type of acid found in wholegrain cereal (phytic acid)

Phytic acid: acid found in wholegrain cereals.
Oxalic acid: acid found in spinach.

For you to do

2 The following meals are served in a restaurant:
a a stir-fry with red meat, peppers, finely sliced cabbage and green vegetables
b pasta dish containing a cheddar cheese sauce and spinach.
Thinking about the interrelationships of nutrients, does each meal have a good combination of ingredients? Explain your answers.

Quick Quiz

Answer true or false.

1 Vitamin B is a fat-soluble vitamin.

2 Beef is a protein food.

3 Soya is an HBV protein food.

4 Starch is a form of carbohydrate.

5 Starch is a polysaccharide.

6 Liver is rich in protein, vitamin A and iron.

7 Sodium is required for strong bones and teeth.

8 Folic acid and iron are both required for healthy blood.

9 Vitamins A, B and C are known as antioxidant vitamins.

10 Vitamin B is required to release energy from foods.

CHAPTER 2: CURRENT DIETARY ADVICE

In this chapter

- Dietary targets
- Ways to meet current dietary targets
- Choice of cooking methods
- Relationship between diet and health
- Food labelling

There will always be questions on current dietary advice in the examination papers at Foundation, General and Credit levels. These questions are always based on the Scottish dietary targets. Remember all the targets listed on page 18 to help with your examination. When a question asks about current dietary advice or healthy eating, it will mean the Scottish dietary targets.

DIETARY TARGETS

Scottish dietary targets were established as part of a 'diet action plan' by the Scottish Office in 1996. They were designed to ensure that the Scottish population had good guidance for a healthy diet. The original aim was to have achieved all of the targets by 2005, and the Scottish Executive has since committed itself to implementation beyond 2005.

The targets identified in the chart on page 18 are designed to provide guidance as to the correct types and quantities of foods that should be eaten in order to promote a healthy diet.

The poor diet of deprived communities is a major reason why they experience such poor health...

from: ***Towards a Healthier Scotland***, Scottish Executive document

Health gap between rich and poor Scots revealed

from: ***Scotsman*** newspaper

Deep Fried Candy Bars: Scotland's Worst Food?

from: ***National Geographic*** magazine

DIETARY TARGET	FOUNDATION	GENERAL	CREDIT
Fruit and vegetables	Advised to eat more.	Intake to double.	Intake to double to at least 400 grams per day.
Bread	Advised to eat more.	Intake to increase, mainly using wholemeal and brown bread.	Intake to increase by 45% from present daily intake.
Breakfast cereal	Advised to eat more.	Intake to double.	Intake to double to 34 grams per day.
Total complex carbohydrates (TCC)	Advised to eat more fruit and vegetables, bread, breakfast cereals, rice and pasta as well as potatoes.	Intake to increase by a quarter through eating more fruit and vegetables, bread, breakfast cereals, rice and pasta as well as potatoes.	Intake to increase by 25% through eating more fruit and vegetables, bread, breakfast cereals, rice and pasta. Potato consumption to increase by 25%.
Fish	Advised to eat more fish, especially oily fish.	Intake of white fish to be maintained. Intake of oily fish to double.	Intake of white fish to be maintained. Intake of oily fish to double from 44 grams per week to 88 grams per week.
Salt	Advised to eat less.	Average intake to reduce.	Average intake to reduce from 163 mmol per day to 100 mmol per day (reduced to 6g per day).
Sugar	Adult intake not to increase. Intake by children to reduce by half.	Adult intake of **non-milk extrinsic (NME) sugars** not to rise. Intake of NME sugars by children to reduce by half.	Adult intake of NME sugars not to rise. Intake of NME sugars by children to reduce by half, i.e. to less than 10% of energy.
Fats	Advised to eat less fat, especially saturated fat.	Average intake of total fat to be reduced. Average intake of saturated fat to be reduced.	Average intake of total fat to be reduced to no more than 35% of food energy. Average intake of saturated fat to be reduced to no more than 11% of food energy.

WORD BANK

Non-milk extrinsic sugar: examples include sugars in honey and table sugar.

CREDIT

Items in colour are not essential for Foundation or General levels. They are helpful to learn for Credit level.

Dietary target for breastfeeding

There is also a dietary target specific to breastfeeding. It is unlikely that you will be able to use this target when adapting meals for people. However, there are sometimes questions linked to specific targets, including breastfeeding.

DIETARY TARGET	FOUNDATION	GENERAL	CREDIT
Breastfeeding	More mothers should breastfeed their babies.	Breastfeeding should be encouraged in the first 6 weeks of a baby's life.	The proportion of mothers breastfeeding their babies in the first 6 weeks of life should increase **to more than 50%**.

Internet activity

1 Visit the BBC website and read the article which provides an update on the progress made towards achieving all of the targets set out above.

a How successful do you think Scotland has been in achieving the Scottish Dietary Targets? Explain your answer.

b What does the article suggest are the main reasons for any lack of progress?

Links to this site and other websites relating to Standard Grade Home Economics can be found at:
www.leckieandleckie.co.uk
by clicking on the Learning Lab button and navigating to the Standard Grade Home Economics Course Notes page.

WAYS TO MEET CURRENT DIETARY TARGETS

It is important to know what the dietary targets are. But it is just as important to know how to adapt food, and different preparation and cooking methods, to help meet the dietary targets.

Ways to increase fish intake
- Use fish instead of meat in certain dishes (e.g. stir fry, fish burgers, risotto).
- Use oily fish such as sardines and mackerel in a wide range of food items (e.g. as a filling for pitta bread or as pizza topping).
- Use fish to make soups and some sauces.
- Use different types of fish for a starter (e.g. prawn cocktail, mackerel pâté).

Ways to increase vegetable intake
- Include a variety of salads and/or vegetables with each meal.
- Add extra vegetables to soups and stews.
- Some vegetables can be used to make healthy drinks as alternatives to sugary fizzy drinks, e.g. smoothies.
- Some vegetables (e.g. carrots, cucumber, celery) can be eaten as snacks or put into packed lunches.
- Many supermarkets now sell small pre-prepared vegetable snack bags, e.g. carrot sticks or baby cucumbers.

Ways to increase TCC intake

- Use rice or pasta instead of chips.
- Make home-made soups using grains and pulses instead of packet soups.
- Use wholemeal flour instead of white flour.
- Use wholegrain breakfast cereals instead of sugar-coated breakfast cereals.

Ways to increase breakfast cereal intake

- Eat a bowl of wholegrain breakfast cereal in the morning or as a snack.
- Use crushed wholegrain breakfast cereals as a topping for pies and desserts.
- Add crushed breakfast cereals to biscuit or scone doughs.
- Use crushed breakfast cereals as a coating for food to be baked or fried.

Ways to increase fruit intake

- Eat fruit as a snack and add it to packed lunches.
- Eat fruit-based puddings instead of jam- or syrup-based puddings.
- Drink fresh fruit juice or fruit smoothies instead of sugary fizzy drinks.
- Add fruit to baked products (e.g. muffins).
- Many supermarkets now sell pre-prepared fruit snacks.

Ways to increase bread intake

- Use wholemeal bread instead of white bread (e.g. in sandwiches, toast).
- Use bread to make healthy puddings (e.g. bread pudding and summer fruit pudding).
- Use wholemeal bread to make breadcrumbs for coating food or to provide bulk for some food items (e.g. beef burgers).
- Some white breads have been specially developed which have added NSP so making them a healthier alternative
- Bread intake can be varied because many different flavoured breads are now available, e.g. bread that has sun-dried tomatoes, olives, garlic, etc. added to give a different taste.

Internet activity

2 Visit the Weetabix website and go to the section of the website marked **Media**. Click on 'The Weetabix Week' video clip. Make a note of the different ways in which this breakfast manufacturer suggests that you can enjoy Weetabix, and comment on how these contribute to a healthy diet.

Links to this site and other websites relating to Standard Grade Home Economics can be found at:

LECKIE&LECKIE
Learning Lab

Ways to reduce fat intake

- Choose lean cuts of meat and trim visible fat from meat.
- Use low-fat products (e.g. low-fat cheese, yoghurt, and salad dressing) where possible.
- Don't add extra fat to food (e.g. glazing vegetables with butter, extra fat added to cooking).
- Skim fat from gravies, soups, stews and mince after cooking.
- Grill meat rather than fry it.

Ways to reduce salt intake

- Reduce the amount of salt added during cooking/do not add salt at the table.
- Use herbs and spices to season rather than salt.
- Use stock cubes and soy sauce sparingly as they have added salt.
- Many savoury snacks have added salt and so should be avoided or low-salt varieties used.
- Use low-salt products if available (there are low-salt alternatives available in supermarkets).

Ways to reduce sugar intake

- Reduce the amount of sugar used in recipes for baking and puddings – use artificial sweetener instead or add some dried fruit for sweetness.
- Eat and drink low-calorie/sugar-free drinks and products.
- Eat fruit as a snack rather than sweets, cake or biscuits.
- Fruit tinned in natural juice is lower in sugar than fruit tinned in syrup.

Alcohol

Alcohol is often used in cookery and is sometimes served along with meals. Alcohol provides a lot of energy and is associated with some health problems. It can also hinder the absorption of some nutrients, such as vitamin B1 (see page 10). Follow these steps to reduce the intake of alcohol:

- when cooking, substitute stock for wine or other alcohol
- use alcohol-free wine and lager in cooking
- drink non- or low-alcohol products or low-calorie soft drinks instead of alcoholic drinks.

HINTS & TIPS

> It is very unlikely that you would be asked to state more than four different ways of adapting foods or menus to meet current dietary targets in an examination question. The information on pages 19–21 will help you with these types of questions.

INGREDIENT/FOOD	ADAPTATION	REASON FOR ADAPTATION
Bread/sandwich/toast	Use wholemeal varieties.	Adds NSP to the diet.
Butter/margarine	Polyunsaturated margarine/low-fat spread.	Reduces fat (including saturated fat) content of diet. Polyunsaturated fat is better for health than saturated fat.
Whole milk	Skimmed or semi-skimmed milk.	Reduces fat (including saturated fat) content of the diet.
Plain flour/Self-raising flour	Wholemeal flour/ wholemeal self-raising flour	Adds NSP to the diet.
Cheddar cheese/cheese	Low-fat cheese/edam.	Reduces fat (including saturated fat) content of the diet.
Sugary drink	Water/low-fat milk/fresh fruit juice.	Reduces the sugar intake of the diet. Milk adds important nutrients (see pages 7–12). Fruit juice helps meet the target for increasing fruit intake.
Snacks (e.g. crisps)	Piece of fruit. Low-fat crisps. Low-salt crisps.	Reduces fat and salt content whilst helping with fruit target. Reduces the fat content of the diet. Reduces the salt content of the diet
Biscuits/cakes	Piece of fruit. Plain biscuit/cake or wholemeal varieties.	Reduces sugar content while helping to meet fruit target. Can reduce the fat and sugar intake. Wholemeal versions also increase NSP content of the diet.
White rice/pasta	Brown rice/brown, green or red pasta.	Increases NSP content. Red and green pasta are made by adding spinach or tomato to the pasta during manufacture and so help towards achieving the vegetable target.

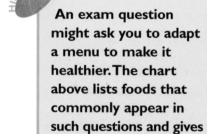

An exam question might ask you to adapt a menu to make it healthier. The chart above lists foods that commonly appear in such questions and gives some suggestions for adaptation to help you.

For you to do

3 Study the ingredients list for a cheese soufflé below. Thinking about the Scottish dietary targets, suggest how they could be adapted to make a healthier version.

- 25 g margarine
- 200 ml full cream milk
- 50 g cheddar cheese
- 25 g plain flour
- 3 eggs
- pinch salt

CHOICE OF COOKING METHODS

As well as adapting the **types** of food you use when preparing meals, choosing appropriate **cooking methods** will also help meet current dietary advice. Not all methods of cooking are suitable for all types of foods. There are some methods of cooking which should be used less frequently because they increase the fat content of the food.

Some methods add fat to foods during cooking.

Some methods of cooking help remove fat.

Some methods remove nutrients from cooking – especially vitamins B and C, which are water-soluble and not stable when subjected to heat.

METHOD OF COOKING	FAT IS ADDED	NO FAT IS ADDED	FAT IS REMOVED	NUTRIENTS ARE LOST
Grilling		●	●	some
Baking		●		some
Boiling		●		some
Shallow frying	●			some
Stir-frying	a little			
Deep frying	●			some
Steaming		●		
Microwave cooking		●		
Pressure cooking		●		
Poaching		●		

Additional factors affect the nutritional quality of the food we prepare and cook, particularly the effects of alkalinity, solubility and heat.

● Alkalinity

- When added to water, this increases the loss of vitamin C.
- Raising agents in some baked foods will reduce the vitamin B1 content.

● Solubility

- Vitamins C and B dissolve in water.

  The vitamins leach out of the food during cooking.
  The water for cooking can be used for soups and sauces as it contains the dissolved nutrients.

- Vitamins A and D are soluble in fat.

  These are lost when fat drips during grilling.

- Cooking in water for a long period of time will cause vitamin loss.
- Cooking in a large amount of water will cause vitamin loss.

● Heat

- Vitamin B is destroyed at high temperatures.
- Vitamin C is sensitive to low temperatures.

☆ Pressure cooking, microwave cooking and steaming may help retain vitamins if used correctly.

RELATIONSHIP BETWEEN DIET AND HEALTH

Eating a diet which meets the Scottish dietary targets will help to develop good health and prevent a wide range of illnesses. There are a number of diseases or health conditions that can be related to poor diet.

Anaemia

Anaemia is mainly caused by:

- not having enough iron (iron deficiency)
- not having enough vitamin B12 (B12 deficiency)
- not having enough folic acid (folic acid deficiency).

Red blood cells contain a substance called **haemoglobin**. This carries oxygen in the blood. Anaemia is caused by a very low level of red cells and haemoglobin. As a result, the oxygen-carrying capacity of the blood is reduced.

The symptoms of anaemia depend on the type of deficiency, as shown in the table below.

Bowel disorders

There are many different types of bowel disorders that are linked to poor diet:

- constipation
- haemorrhoids (piles)
- cancer
- diverticular disease.

Constipation

This is the passage of hard and dry faeces (bowel movements) fewer than two or three times a week, associated with an uncomfortable abdominal feeling. The most common causes of constipation are a relative lack of NSP and liquids in the diet. The main treatment is a diet with enough NSP content (up to 35 grams a day, then reducing to 18 grams per day).

Haemorrhoids (piles)

These are enlarged and **engorged** (swollen) blood vessels in or around the back passage (anus), which may be associated with pain, bleeding, itching and feeling as if a lump or bump is hanging down. Piles are very common, especially in countries where the diet is highly processed and low in NSP.

TYPE OF ANAEMIA	SYMPTOMS
Iron-deficient anaemia (the most common form).	<ul><li>tiredness</li><li>breathlessness</li><li>dizziness (especially when standing) and a weak, rapid pulse</li></ul>
Vitamin B12-deficient anaemia (normally called megaloblastic anaemia). Vitamin B12 is found only in animal products and so can be deficient in vegan diets.	<ul><li>damage to nerves (abnormal sensation and movement)</li><li>sore tongue</li><li>pigmented skin</li><li>colour blindness</li><li>depression, confusion and decreased intellectual function</li></ul>
Folic acid-deficient anaemia. (Folic acid is important in the development of the fetus, and is important for women intending to become pregnant as well as during pregnancy.)	<ul><li>fetal malformations (including spina bifida)</li><li>neurological abnormalities in infants</li></ul>

People most at risk of developing piles are those who have raised abdominal pressure, such as:

- those chronically straining with constipation
- women during or after pregnancy
- people who are overweight.

Piles are very common but can be prevented by:

- avoiding becoming overweight
- eating a diet high in NSP
- exercising regularly.

Cancer

The body is made up of many types of cells. Normally cells grow, divide, and produce more cells as they are needed to keep the body healthy and functioning properly. Sometimes, however, the process goes wrong and cells keep dividing when new cells are not needed. This leads to a tumour or **cancer**.

The colon and rectum are parts of the body's digestive system which remove nutrients from food and store waste until it passes out of the body. Colorectal cancer (cancers of the colon and/or rectum) seems to be associated with diets that are high in fat and calories and low in NSP.

A diet rich in fruit, vegetables and wholegrain cereals will provide the body with vitamins A, C and E, as well as providing NSP. All of these substances have roles in preventing the development of cancer, especially bowel cancer (see pages 9–10).

Other diet-related cancers of the digestive system

- Consumption of large amounts of pickled, smoked or salted foods large has been shown to have a link to the development of some types of cancer of the digestive system.
- Drinking large amounts of alcohol appears to increase the chance of developing certain types of cancer.

Advice: eat these foods and drink alcohol in moderation.

Diverticular disease

Diverticular disease (also known as **diverticulosis**) is a condition in which small sacs or pouches called **diverticula** form in the wall of the large intestine. These diverticula can become infected, leading to a condition known as **diverticulitis**.

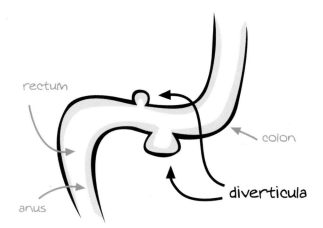

Diverticular disease is common in elderly people in developed nations. It is rare in people under 20 years of age or in developing countries.

The main cause of diverticular disease is believed to be long-standing constipation. The large intestine produces solid stools; constipation increases pressure within the intestine and over many years this weakens small areas of the lining of the intestine and allows small sacs to form.

Medicine can be used to treat diverticular disease, but there are also simple steps that can be followed to help prevent the disease and its complications. Many of these measures involve following a healthy diet and lifestyle and taking steps to prevent constipation:

- stick to a healthy, high-NSP, low-fat diet containing plenty of fruit, vegetables, wholemeal bread and wholegrain cereals
- avoid constipating foods such as bananas and rice
- drink at least two litres of water per day
- undertake regular daily exercise to stimulate circulation (it is thought that a sluggish circulation may aggravate diverticular disease).

Coronary heart disease

The heart needs a supply of blood to function correctly. **Coronary heart disease** (CHD) occurs when fatty deposits stick to the artery walls and block the arteries that provide the heart with its supply of blood. This can lead to severe chest pain, a heart attack and possibly death. **Cholesterol** is one of the components of this fatty deposit.

Cholesterol is a soft, waxy substance found among the fats in the bloodstream and in all your body's cells. It is an important part of a healthy body because it is used to form cell membranes, some hormones and other tissues in the body.

The level of cholesterol in the blood is linked to the development of these fatty deposits. If the level of cholesterol is high, the risk of CHD is generally high.

The amount of cholesterol in the blood is increased by eating the wrong types of foods. Saturated fatty acids can raise blood cholesterol, which increases your risk of heart disease. Salt has also been shown to have a link with CHD (see hypertension section below).

There are other risk factors associated with CHD, as well as bad diet:

- cigarette smoking
- insufficient exercise
- family history
- high blood pressure
- alcohol consumption.
- stress
- obesity
- age
- gender

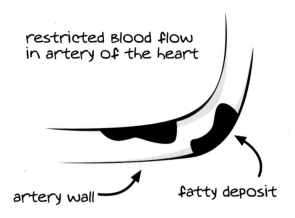

restricted blood flow in artery of the heart

artery wall

fatty deposit

Steps that may prevent certain CHD
- Reduce the intake of saturated fat in the diet.
- Increasing the amount of antioxidants (vitamins A, C and E) in the diet may help to prevent CHD by stopping the fatty deposits from sticking to artery walls.
- Changing from a diet high in saturated fat to one that is based mainly on polyunsaturated fat may be beneficial. It is thought that polyunsaturated fatty acids may help reduce the tendency for blood to clot and so reduce the risk of heart attack.

The interrelationship between all these factors makes this a disease that can affect anyone at any time. But a man who smokes, drinks and does not exercise is likely to be at a higher risk of CHD than one who has fewer risk factors. Similarly, a woman who smokes, drinks and is overweight will be at a higher risk than someone who doesn't smoke or drink or is of normal weight.

Hypertension and strokes

Hypertension is another name for **high blood pressure**. High blood pressure directly increases the risk of CHD (which leads to heart attacks) and **strokes**, especially if other risk factors are present. High blood pressure can lead to the thickening and hardening of artery walls, which causes the heart to work harder than normal to pump blood around the body. As a result, both the heart and arteries are more prone to injury.

If high blood pressure isn't treated, the heart may have to work harder and harder to pump enough blood and oxygen around the body's organs and tissues to meet their needs. When the heart is forced to work harder than normal for an extended time, it tends to enlarge and weaken.

Arterial damage is harmful because hardened or narrowed arteries may not be able to carry enough blood to meet the needs of the body's organs. If the body's organs don't get enough oxygen and nutrients, they can't work properly.

Normal artery
with good
blood flow

Artery with
fatty deposits
leading to increased
blood pressure
and possible risk of
blood clot

Another risk is that a blood clot may lodge in an artery narrowed by fatty deposits, which then deprives part of the body of its normal blood supply. This can lead to a stroke, where the blood supply to the brain is interrupted or stopped.

There are a number of factors that contribute to high blood pressure. Two factors relate to the diet:

- **diet rich in sodium (salt):** high sodium consumption increases the blood pressure of some people, leading to high blood pressure. People diagnosed with high blood pressure are often put on sodium-restricted diets.
- **being overweight or obese:** studies have shown that changes in blood pressure levels are related to body weight. People who are overweight are more likely to have high blood pressure.

Other risk factors associated with high blood pressure are:

- age and gender (below 55 years of age the risk is higher for men, but above 55 it is higher for women)
- family history
- alcohol
- race (Africans are at more risk of high blood pressure than Caucasians)
- some medicines
- lack of exercise.

Weight control and obesity

In the UK, being overweight is a common problem. Look at the headline:

Child obesity soars in UK...

from: **BBC News** *website*

Being overweight is not itself a common cause of death; however, it does increase the risk of a variety of medical conditions:

- CHD
- stroke
- certain cancers.
- diabetes
- gallstones

We all need energy for our bodies to function correctly. Even when sleeping, our bodies need energy to function. If you are very energetic, you will need more energy than if you are not. However, if you do not use all the energy that you consume in food, the extra is stored in the body as fat.

The only way to lose weight is to ensure that you use more energy than you take in. The best ways to do this are:

- to eat fewer energy-rich foods – particularly fatty foods
- to take more exercise – which will burn extra energy.

Steps to prevent obesity

- Fat is a concentrated source of energy so eat fewer high-fat foods (e.g. pies, cakes, confectionery).
- Reduce intake of sugary foods as they provide lots of energy but few other nutrients.
- Eat a low-energy diet, formed in part by starchy foods, fruits and vegetables, lean meat and low-fat dairy products.
- Eat foods high in NSP in order to feel fuller for a longer period of time, reduce feelings of hunger, and so reduce the desire to eat.

Obesity: a condition of being excessively overweight.

Body mass index (BMI): a calculation that indicates whether an individual is roughly a healthy weight for their height.

Body mass index

4   Visit the Weightconcern website. Select the Child Body Mass Index (BMI) Calculator link on the left-hand side of the home page, and fill in these details to find out the BMI of each boy:

	Christopher		Ryan
●	Age: 14	●	Age: 14
●	Sex: male	●	Sex: male
●	Weight: 45 kg	●	Weight: 35 kg
●	Height: 150 cm	●	Height: 110 cm

a   What is the BMI for each of Christopher and Ryan?

b   Is this good or bad for each? Explain.

c   You can take your own height and weight and complete the calculator if you wish

Links to this site and other websites relating to Standard Grade Home Economics can be found at:

Tooth decay

Tooth decay is sometimes called **dental caries**.

When you eat, bits of food (some too small for you to see) remain in your mouth. They feed bacteria that grow in **plaque** (a sticky film that forms on the surface of teeth). Plaque is the main cause of tooth decay and gum disease. Bacteria produce acid which dissolves teeth, causing tooth decay. Brushing your teeth after meals and after between-meal snacks not only gets rid of the food particles that you can see but also removes plaque from your teeth. Using fluoride toothpaste is important because the

fluoride can help kill bacteria, as well as make your teeth stronger.

However, diet is also important in preventing tooth decay. If your diet is low in certain nutrients, it may be harder for the tissues of your mouth to resist infection. This may be a contributing factor to gum disease, the main cause of tooth loss in adults.

A well-balanced diet will help maintain dental health. When you do snack, avoid soft, sweet, sticky foods, such as cakes, candy and dried fruits, that cling to your teeth and promote tooth decay. Instead, choose foods such as nuts, raw vegetables, plain yoghurt, cheese, unsalted and non-sweetened popcorn and sugarless gum or candy.

FOOD LABELLING

To the consumer, food labelling can be confusing, especially when trying to choose foods that can help meet current dietary advice. Many use words like 'pure' and 'natural', but what does this really mean? There are laws and guidelines which mean that a standard format for nutrition labelling must be followed.

The information on a label allows you to compare the nutritive value of similar products. So what should you look for? Look at the example opposite.

At present, nutrition labelling is voluntary unless a manufacturer makes a specific nutritional claim about the product on the packet or in an advert (e.g. 'low-fat cheese').

The ingredients in a food product **must** be displayed on its food label. However, it is not always easy to understand what the listed ingredients are. For example, the following ingredients may appear on a label:

sucrose   **lactose**   **glucose syrup**

These are all forms of sugar. If you do not know this, then you probably won't realise this product contains sugar.

The Food Standards Agency, a body of the UK Government, has developed a new set of guidelines for the labelling of food. These voluntary guidelines use 'traffic lights' to make it easier for consumers to

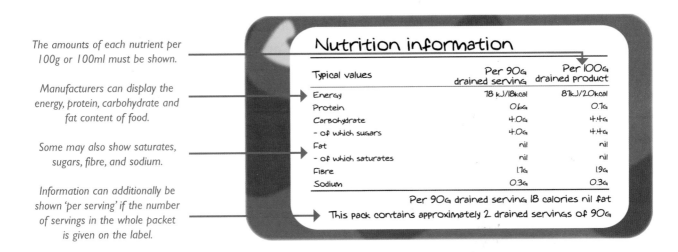

The amounts of each nutrient per 100g or 100ml must be shown.

Manufacturers can display the energy, protein, carbohydrate and fat content of food.

Some may also show saturates, sugars, fibre, and sodium.

Information can additionally be shown 'per serving' if the number of servings in the whole packet is given on the label.

Nutrition information

Typical values	Per 90g drained serving	Per 100g drained product
Energy	78 kJ/18kcal	87kJ/20kcal
Protein	0.6g	0.7g
Carbohydrate	4.0g	4.4g
– of which sugars	4.0g	4.4g
Fat	nil	nil
– of which saturates	nil	nil
Fibre	1.7g	1.9g
Sodium	0.3g	0.3g

Per 90g drained serving 18 calories nil fat
This pack contains approximately 2 drained servings of 90g

choose healthy foods. However, some manufacturers have rejected this system and developed a second labelling scheme based on 'guideline daily amounts'.

The Traffic Light labelling system

The **Traffic Light** system was developed by the Food Standards Agency and is based on the colours used in traffic lights.

Remember that in order to follow current dietary advice we should:

- reduce our fat (particularly saturated fat) intake
- reduce our sugar intake
- reduce our salt intake.

The Traffic Light system allow you to see at a glance if a food has a:

The Traffic Light system will indicate the amount of sugar/salt/fat either per serving or per 100 g of the food.

So if you see a **red** light on the front of the packet, you know that the food contains a high amount of something that we should be cutting down on. This does not mean that you should not buy the food, but remember not to buy or eat too many foods with red lights.

When looking at foods on a supermarket shelf, you might be faced with many different traffic light colours, even on the same product. Try to select those products that display more **green** and **amber** lights.

Here are some examples of foods displaying traffic light symbols:

high amount of fat / sugar / salt

medium amount of fat / sugar / salt

low amount of fat / sugar / salt

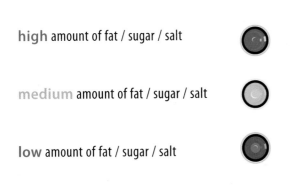

prawn mayo sandwich

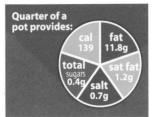

houmous

The Guideline Daily Amount labelling system

The alternative scheme launched by major food manufacturers and retailers is called the **Guideline Daily Amount** (GDA) system. The GDA system is based on recommended guideline amounts of different nutrients that a person should eat every day in order to achieve a balanced diet.

The label below shows how the GDA works.

Sugars, fat, saturates and salt:
- *the amount in grams shows how much of each nutrient there is in a portion*
- *the percentage sign shows how much of your daily GDA for each nutrient is provided by one portion*

The top line refers to the specified portion or serving size whether in grams or millilitres.

This figure tells you how many calories there are in one serving or portion of the food.

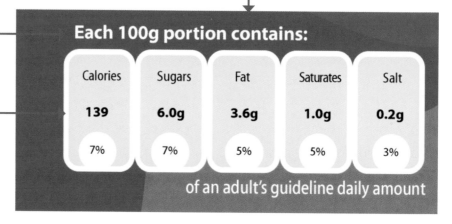

Each 100g portion contains:				
Calories	Sugars	Fat	Saturates	Salt
139	6.0g	3.6g	1.0g	0.2g
7%	7%	5%	5%	3%

of an adult's guideline daily amount

Notes
The figures refer to a woman of healthy weight undertaking moderate activity and exercise, so are not as accurate for men. Children's GDAs are used on products targeted at children.

Internet activity

5 Visit the Eatwell page of the Food Standards Agency website. Watch some of the short adverts promoting the Traffic Light labelling system. How well do they explain the system?

6 Visit the Orange News website. Read the article and watch the short video about the arguments for and against the different labelling schemes being promoted by the Food Standards Agency and the food manufacturers.

Links to these sites and other websites relating to Standard Grade Home Economics can be found at: (LECKIE&LECKIE Learning Lab)

For you to do

7 Collect three different food packages which display the Traffic Light labelling system. Explain how each food would or would not help the consumer to meet current dietary advice.

8 Study the two food products and answer the questions that follow.

pizza

pasta

Each 180g serving contains:				
Calories	Sugars	Fat	Saturates	Salt
458	4.2g	18.6g	7.8g	2.3g
23%	5%	27%	39%	38%
of an adult's guideline daily amount				

Each 200g serving contains:				
Calories	Sugars	Fat	Saturates	Salt
319	9.3g	8.0g	1.5g	1.6g
16%	10%	11%	8%	27%
of an adult's guideline daily amount				

a Which product has the lower percentage of salt?

b Which product would be better for someone on a low-fat diet?

c Which product would be worse for developing tooth decay?

d Which product would be better for a person on a high-energy diet?

e How many calories does the pizza contain?

f How many calories does the pizza contain for a 360 g serving?

g How many grams of salt does the average serving of the pasta dish contain?

Quick Quiz

Answer true or false.

1 We are advised to eat more fresh vegetables.

2 Children should eat more oily fish.

3 Vitamins A, C and E can help in the prevention of certain types of cancers.

4 Some nutrients are lost during the baking of foods.

5 Anaemia is an illness caused by a lack of NSP in the diet.

6 A high-salt diet can lead to high blood pressure.

7 A low-fat diet can lead to coronary heart disease.

8 Semi-skimmed milk has a low-saturated fat content.

9 TCC stands for Total Carbohydrate Content.

10 People who are overweight have an increased chance of suffering from piles.

CHAPTER 3: INDIVIDUALS HAVE VARYING DIETARY NEEDS

In this chapter

- Dietary requirements of different groups of individuals
- Dietary requirements of groups with special needs
- Factors affecting food choice

DIETARY REQUIREMENTS OF DIFFERENT GROUPS OF INDIVIDUALS

No two people are alike. We all have different dietary requirements. There are, however, certain groups in society who have specific dietary needs.

The needs of individuals and groups in society are measured by **Dietary Reference Values** (DRVs). These are outlined in the charts on pages 33–38 for different population groups. DRVs are subdivided into:

- **Reference Nutrient Intake** (RNI): the amount of a nutrient that is sufficient for most of the population
- **Estimated Average Requirement** (EAR): estimate of the average need for a nutrient. Some may need more, some may need less.
- **Lower Reference Nutrient Intake** (LRNI): for those people who have lower nutrient needs.

Infants

An infant's diet for the first few weeks of life is milk (whether breast or bottle-fed). Human milk is ideal for a number of reasons:

- it contains the correct composition and proportion of nutrients to ensure growth and development
- it is of the correct temperature and consistency
- the milk is easy to digest
- it is free and convenient
- it contains **antibodies** that can help fight infection
- no preparation is required and so risk of contamination from bacteria is reduced
- breast-feeding helps develop a bond between mother and child.

WORD BANK

Antibody: a type of protein produced in the blood which fights diseases by attacking and killing harmful bacteria.

AGE RANGE	EAR	REFERENCE NUTRIENT INTAKE									
	Energy (kcal/day)	Protein (g/day)	Vitamin A (retinol equiv. µg/day)	Thiamin (mg/day)	Riboflavin (mg/day)	Niacin (nicotinic acid equiv. mg/day)	Vitamin C (mg/day)	Vitamin D (µg/day)	Calcium (mg/day)	Iron (mg/day)	Sodium (mg/day)
Boys < 1	545 – 920	12.5 – 14.9	350	0.2 – 0.3	0.4	3 – 5	25	8.5 (0 – 6 mths)	525	1.7 – 7.8	210 – 350
Girls < 1	515 – 865	12.5 – 14.9	350	0.2 – 0.3	0.4	3 – 5	25	8.5 (0 – 6 mths)	525	1.7 – 7.8	210 – 350

Children

As childhood is a time of fast growth and development there is an increased demand for all nutrients.

NUTRIENT	DIETARY NEED
Protein	Protein is required for the growth, maintenance and repair of body tissues.
Total complex carbohydrate	This is a period of activity and children will require energy. To meet current dietary targets, starchy carbohydrates should be the main source of energy. All children require a source of fat. Children under five should not be given skimmed milk as it has a lower fat content and less of the fat-soluble vitamins (A and D).
Calcium, vitamin D and phosphorus	As this is a period of growth and development, calcium, vitamin D and phosphorus are required to ensure correct bone development.
Iron	Iron is essential for healthy blood. Increased activity means the body's cells require more oxygen. This is carried by the red blood cells, which need iron to carry the oxygen.
Vitamin C	Essential for absorption of iron as well as for maintaining the body's connective tissue.
Fluoride	To ensure protection for developing teeth.

AGE RANGE	EAR	REFERENCE NUTRIENT INTAKE										
	Energy (kcal/day)	Protein (g/day)	Vitamin A (retinol equiv. µg/day)	Thiamin (mg/day)	Riboflavin (mg/day)	Niacin (nicotinic acid equiv. mg/day)	Vitamin C (mg/day)	Vitamin D (µg/day)	Calcium (mg/day)	Iron (mg/day)	Sodium (mg/day)
Boys 1–3	1230	14.5	400	0.5	0.6	8	30	7.0 (6 mths – 3 yrs)	350	6.9	500
Boys 4–6	1715	19.7	500	0.7	0.8	11	30	–	450	6.1	700
Boys 7–10	1970	28.3	500	0.7	1.0	12	30	–	550	8.7	1200
Girls 1–3	1165	14.5	400	0.5	0.6	8	30	7.0 (6 mths – 3 yrs)	350	6.9	500
Girls 4–6	1545	19.7	500	0.7	0.8	11	30	–	450	6.1	700
Girls 7–10	1740	28.3	500	0.7	1.0	12	30	–	550	8.7	1200

Adolescents

This is a period of rapid growth and body development. For this reason, nutritional requirements will increase. In particular, the following nutrients will be important.

WORD BANK

Menstruation: the monthly discharge of blood and other matter from a non-pregnant woman's uterus.

NUTRIENT	DIETARY NEED
Protein	This is a period of sometimes rapid growth and so protein is required for the growth, maintenance and repair of body tissues.
Carbohydrate	Due to the larger body frame at this time of development, energy requirements will increase. Energy needs will vary from individual to individual depending on how active they are.
Iron	This is important for teenage girls in particular who, due to the onset of **menstruation**, will require increased sources of iron to prevent anaemia. Boys also require iron as blood volume increases during this time of fast growth.

AGE RANGE	EAR	REFERENCE NUTRIENT INTAKE										
	Energy (kcal/day)	Protein (g/day)	Vitamin A (retinol equiv. µg/day)	Thiamin (mg/day)	Riboflavin (mg/day)	Niacin (nicotinic acid equiv. mg/day)	Vitamin C (mg/day)	Vitamin D (µg/day)	Calcium (mg/day)	Iron (mg/day)	Sodium (mg/day)
Boys 11–14	2200	42.1	600	0.9	1.2	15	35	–	1000	11.3	1600
Boys 15–18	2755	55.2	700	1.1	1.3	18	40	–	1000	11.3	1600
Girls 11–14	1845	41.2	600	0.7	1.1	12	35	–	800	14.8	1600
Girls 15–18	2110	45.4	600	0.8	1.1	14	40	–	800	14.8	1600

Adults

At this stage, body growth has declined so nutrients are required for maintenance and repair purposes. Individual nutrient requirements will depend on a variety of individual factors, discussed in the next section.

AGE RANGE	EAR	REFERENCE NUTRIENT INTAKE										
	Energy (kcal/day)	Protein (g/day)	Vitamin A (retinol equiv. µg/day)	Thiamin (mg/day)	Riboflavin (mg/day)	Niacin (nicotinic acid equiv. mg/day)	Vitamin C (mg/day)	Vitamin D (µg/day)	Calcium (mg/day)	Iron (mg/day)	Sodium (mg/day)
Men 19–50	2550	55.5	700	1.0	1.3	17	40	–	700	8.7	1600
Men 50+	2550	53.3	700	0.9	1.3	16	40	(65+ µg/day)	700	8.7	1600
Women 19–50	1940	45	600	0.8	1.1	13	40	–	700	14.8	1600
Women 50+	1900	46.5	600	0.8	1.1	12	40	(65+ µg/day)	700	8.7	1600

Energy requirements of both males and females reduce from teenage years as their rate of body growth and development decreases.

The requirement for iron decreases as the menstrual loss of blood stops.

Elderly people

Elderly people generally become less active, requiring less energy than when they were younger. It is important to ensure that meals are still well-planned and balanced to ensure that the correct nutrients are available in the correct proportions for the maintenance and repair of the body. There are a number of diet-related problems that can occur in later life.

DIET-RELATED PROBLEM	DIETARY ADVICE
Constipation	The diet should have an adequate amount of NSP. It is also important that sufficient liquid is consumed.
Anaemia	The diet should have sufficient sources of iron and vitamin C.
Bone disorders	A diet rich in calcium, vitamin D and phosphorus is advised to prevent bone disorders.
Digestive problems	Some elderly people have false teeth, which can make chewing some foods difficult. With careful planning of meals such problems can be overcome.
	Digesting fatty foods can be a problem. Foods and cooking methods should be selected carefully.

For you to do

1 **a** Explain why the energy needs of boys are greater then energy needs of girls.
   b Explain why teenage girls require more iron than teenage boys.
   c Explain why the energy needs of women decrease with age.
   d Explain why the protein needs of both men and women decrease with age.

DIETARY REQUIREMENTS OF GROUPS WITH SPECIAL NEEDS

A number of groups of people have particular dietary requirements, including pregnant women, vegetarians and vegans.

Pregnant women

It is important that women who are planning to become pregnant or are already pregnant follow a healthy balanced diet.

Many women find that constipation and piles occur during pregnancy. A diet rich in NSP and with sufficient intake of liquids will help prevent such problems.

CREDIT

Bone disorders
Osteoporosis is a disease in which bones become fragile and more likely to break. Women are more likely than men to develop this disease. There is no cure, but it can be prevented by following a balanced diet rich in calcium and vitamin D, exercising using light weights and by following a healthy lifestyle with no smoking or excessive alcohol use.

Osteomalacia means 'soft bones'. This softening is caused by the loss of calcium from the skeleton. This has a number of causes, one of which is poor diet, particularly related to vitamin D deficiency.

NUTRIENT	DIETARY NEED
Protein	Additional protein will be required for the development of the fetus's body cells.
Carbohydrate	In the last three months of pregnancy, the body has a greater requirement for energy. This is a time of rapid growth and movement for the developing fetus. It is important, however, not to take in too much energy, otherwise additional weight gain may occur and this can lead to complications.
Iron	The loss of blood via menstruation ceases during pregnancy so an increased intake of iron is not considered necessary. It is important, however, that iron intake is maintained as this will supply the newly born baby with sufficient iron to last it through the first few weeks of life.
Vitamin C	Foods rich in vitamin C should be in the diet to enable iron to be absorbed. Extra vitamin C is needed to help the baby's tissue formation.
Folic acid	It is important that sufficient foods containing folic acid are consumed before and during pregnancy – especially in the first three months. Folic acid reduces the risk of babies being born with neural tube defects such as spina bifida. Folic acid supplements may be advised by a doctor or midwife.
Calcium, vitamin D and phosphorus	A baby's bones contain about 30g of calcium at the time of birth. This calcium is provided by the mother's diet. It is important that calcium intake is maintained to ensure that calcium deposits from the mother's bones are not used for this purpose.

Food safety in pregnancy

Some foods should be avoided during pregnancy. For example, liver and liver pâté contain rich amounts of vitamin A. Although the body requires vitamin A for healthy skin and vision, too much can be harmful to the developing baby.

Other foods that should also be avoided during pregnancy include soft cheeses (such as Brie and Camembert), pâté, and cook-chill foods. These products may contain *listeria* bacteria, which can harm the developing baby.

Other foods such as raw eggs (and foods containing raw eggs) may contain *salmonella* bacteria, which can harm a developing baby.

Vegetarians

There are many different types of vegetarians. There are two main types that you have to know about:

- **lactovegetarians**: do not eat meat or meat products, including eggs and fish, but do eat milk, cheese and other dairy products
  - **lacto ovo vegetarians** are a subgroup of lactovegetarians: they *do* eat eggs
- **vegans**: do not eat any animal-derived products, including eggs, milk, cheese and other dairy products.

Within the group of vegetarians, there are smaller sub-groups with more limited diets, such as:

- **pescatarians:** people who do not eat meat or animal flesh but will eat fish. Many people opt for this diet for health reasons.
- **fruitarians:** people who eat only fruits, nuts and seeds. This excludes root plants, such as carrots and potatoes.

There are different reasons why people become vegetarian.

REASON	EXPLANATION
Religion	Some religions have rules about the types of foods that can be eaten. For some religions these rules can be very strict. Many Hindus and Buddhists are vegetarians, although eating some forms of meat is not actually forbidden.
Moral issues	Some people believe that it is wrong to kill animals for food. Others believe that it is not environmentally friendly to use animals for food, as it is an expensive way to produce food.
Health	Some people may follow a vegetarian diet for health-related reasons.
Taste	Some people do not like the taste or texture of meat.
Peer pressure	Some people – particularly younger people – may become vegetarian as a result of pressure from friends.

For whatever reason a person becomes a vegetarian, there are a number of factors that they need to consider when planning meals to ensure that they do not become deficient in certain nutrients.

Lacto vegetarian

- Should have few problems achieving a balanced diet, as three protein foods are still available in the diet.

- Can obtain most nutrients from plant sources except for vitamin B12. Foods which are fortified (have nutrients added to them) with vitamin B12 should be consumed.

Vegan

- Protein is found in varying amounts in plant sources. As these will be LBV proteins, a combination must be taken to make up the shortage of essential amino acids in each.

- Calcium may be deficient – this can be provided by pulses, nuts and fruits and vegetables. The presence of phytic acid may make some calcium unavailable to the body.

- Vitamin D is found in few plant foods. Sunlight is an important source.

- For vegans, the higher intake of NSP will have a positive effect on health, as more pulses, nuts, fruits and vegetables are consumed. The saturated fat content of the diet should also reduce as more polyunsaturated fats are consumed. A vegan diet may also increase the TCC intake of the diet.

Soya can be used to make textured vegetable protein and Tofu. This is a plant source of protein, but has a HBV protein content. It is ideal for inclusion in a vegetarian diet.

Available in pieces, minced and in many foods such as burgers, sausages and ready meals, making it very useful for the diet of a vegetarian.

Mycoprotein (e.g. Quorn) is made from a plant source and is ideal for most vegetarian diets*. It is high in protein, low in fat and is a source of NSP.

*Mycoprotein often uses egg albumen as a binder and so may be not be suitable for some vegetarians.

For you to do

2 Certain groups in society have special dietary requirements. Match up the statements below providing details of the dietary needs of different groups of individuals.

STATEMENT 1		STATEMENT 2	
1	I am anaemic.	A	I eat less now that I'm not as active as I was.
2	I am a pregnant woman.	B	I need to eat more protein-rich foods.
3	I am an elderly person.	C	I need to eat foods rich in iron.
4	RNI	D	I have greater energy needs than girls.
5	I am a lacto ovo vegetarian.	E	I use mycoprotein in my recipes.
6	I am a teenage boy.	F	Amount of nutrient needed by most people.
7	I am a vegan.	G	I do not use mycoprotein in my diet.
8	EAR	H	I need less iron in my diet than when I was younger.
9	I am a 6 week old baby.	I	Average nutrient needs for a group of people.
10	I am a woman aged 65.	J	I need special milk that is easy to digest.

FACTORS AFFECTING FOOD CHOICE

There are a number of common factors that affect the dietary requirements and choice of food for individuals, other than those specifically described above.

Body size

Not everyone has the same body size. We all know people who can eat lots of food but still remain slim. We all know people who just need to look at a cream cake, and the pounds seem to pile on! The amount of energy a person needs is determined by their **basal metabolic rate** (BMR). This is the amount of energy needed when the body is resting, and energy is only required to keep the body functioning – to keep the heart pumping and the lungs breathing. Tall, thin people have higher BMRs. People with a lot of fatty tissue tend to have a lower BMR. Those with a higher BMR will burn energy quickly.

Age

Our nutritional requirements vary as we grow and develop. BMR is higher when we are younger because age brings less lean body mass and slows the BMR. As well as energy differences, the amounts of other nutrients we need will change throughout our lives, as discussed in the previous section. As we age, we generally become less active so our energy requirements become lower.

Gender (male or female)

Men tend to have larger body sizes and so require more protein for the development of additional muscle tissue. Because of this larger body size, energy requirements are greater.

Available income

The amount of income available for purchasing food and food preparation equipment significantly affects the quantity and the type and quality of food, and therefore affects the intake of nutrients. Higher earners generally have a higher intake of animal protein. These foods tend to be higher in saturated fats, for example, which can have long-term health effects. Where income is limited, people tend to eat less fresh fruit and vegetables, because they are often seen as expensive foods and indeed availability of fresh fruits and vegetables may be an issue. Many low-cost foods tend to be high in salt, sugar and saturated fat because adding these is a relatively cheap way to enhance or improve the flavour of the foods.

Health

There are a number of health factors that affect dietary requirements and food choice. We have already looked at pregnancy and vegetarianism. However, there are other health factors that should be considered.

In your Standard Grade Home Economics exam, you may be asked to evaluate the diet of a specific person. Remember to:

- **think about the activities that the person will be involved in**
- **think about each of the major nutrients as well as NSP**
- **think about the function of each nutrient**
- **decide whether this person will need an additional requirement or not**

- **think what might happen to the person if they did not get enough of each nutrient**
- **think about what might happen to the person if they got too much of each nutrient.**

The key to success in these types of questions is to know the sources and functions of all the nutrients.

• Lactation

- Milk is produced to enable a mother to breast-feed her baby.

- Protein, calcium, vitamins A, C, B and D and iron are all important.

- A higher energy and nutrient intake is required.

- Increased water intake is advised.

• Invalids

- People who are immobile (e.g. confined to a bed) will require less energy.

- The requirement for nutrients to maintain and repair body tissues becomes important – protein, calcium, iron and vitamins A, D and C for example.

- Sugar, fat and large amounts of starchy carbohydrates should be avoided.

• Diets

- Medically approved diets (e.g. low cholesterol diets) should always be followed.

- Medical advice should be sought before entering into a slimming diet to ensure the correct balance of nutrients is taken.

Internet research

3 Celebrities and famous people sometimes follow 'fad' diets in order to lose weight. As a result many people copy them and follow such diets. Visit the Weight Loss Resources website, and find out information about some of the diets they mention, such as the Atkins diet or the Cabbage soup diet. Explain why following these diets may not be good for your health in the long term.

Links to this site and other websites relating to Standard Grade Home Economics can be found at:

LECKIE&LECKIE
Learning Lab

> **HINTS & TIPS**
>
> Do not undertake any 'fad' type diet such as those mentioned on the website without consulting your doctor. Following such diets can have serious medical side-effects.

Lifestyle/activities/occupation

The amount of energy people use in physical activity varies according to their occupation, lifestyle and the activities they are involved in.

Active people

- Need more energy to allow muscles to receive the required amounts of energy to function well.
- Need more protein for growth, maintenance and repair of body tissues.
- Need B vitamins to release energy from carbohydrates and fats.
- Need iron and vitamin C to allow oxygen to be transported to the body tissues.
- Need an increased number of antioxidant vitamins to protect cells and tissues during exercise.
- Need extra fluids to replace those lost during perspiration.

Less active people

- Need fewer energy-rich foods during the working day, as their jobs are not physically demanding.
- Have no increased requirements for other nutrients during the working day.
- Although the person may have a non-physical job, he or she may be involved in active hobbies. This will affect their nutritional requirement.

Snickers pie

'Snickers pie', a dessert treat for children created by the celebrity chef Antony Worrall Thompson, has been described as one of the most unhealthy recipes ever published.

The pie contains five Snickers bars with mascarpone, eggs, sugar, soft cheese and puff pastry. One slice of the pie has more than 1,250 calories (more than 2½ times the recommended daily energy intake for 5–6 year olds). The calorie count of a single slice of Snickers pie is about the same as: seven hot dogs or five ring doughnuts.

To do to burn off 1,250 calories you would have to:

- cycle for over 5 hours
- dance for 5½ hours
- play basketball or run for over 3 hours
- play football for over 3½ hours.

For you to do

4   There are many different reasons why people eat some foods and not others. Read the numbered list of statements below and decide (using the abbreviations provided) which is the most likely reason for them not eating a particular food.

Reasons:
- Religious or cultural, RC
- Personal (like/dislike), P
- Health, H
- Moral, M
- Income, I

1   I am a Hindu and I do not eat beef.
2   I only eat organic fruits and vegetables.
3   I am on a diet and will eat only low-fat foods.
4   I cannot eat shellfish because they bring me out in a rash.
5   I do not buy organic foods because of the cost.
6   I have hypertension and need to eat low-salt foods.
7   I do not buy foods which come from Zimbabwe.
8   I do not like the taste of meat and so I am a vegetarian.
9   I do not agree with killing animals for meat and so I am a vegetarian.
10 I am Jewish and so do not eat pork.

Quick Quiz

1   What do the initials RNI stand for?
2   Children under 5 should drink skimmed milk. True or false?
3   Why do adolescents require a high amount of protein?
4   Which two nutrients are important in the prevention of anaemia?
5   Name three foods that it might not be safe for a pregnant woman to eat.
6   What foods does a lacto ovo vegetarian not eat?
7   Name one religion that might encourage a vegetarian diet.
8   What is mycoprotein?
9   The more income you have, the better your diet. True or false?
10 The higher a person's BMR the less energy they burn. True or false?

CHAPTER 4: CLEANLINESS IS IMPORTANT IN RELATION TO HEALTH

In this chapter

- General personal hygiene
- Clothes care
- Hygiene in relation to food handling
- Causes, effects and control of food spoilage
- Food storage and preservation
- Food poisoning
- Preventing food spoilage, contamination and poisoning
- Refrigerators and freezers

GENERAL PERSONAL HYGIENE

Good personal hygiene is important as it helps to boost your self-confidence and make you feel good. It also helps to create a good impression with other people. Good personal hygiene is all about **taking care of your body**.

Bacteria are **organisms** that live all around us. They are so small that they cannot be seen by the naked eye. Bacteria live and grow on our bodies, but we cannot see them. Your skin has tiny **pores** (holes), which help to get rid of waste products from the body. Bacteria can thrive on these waste products. The end result of this is that your skin may begin to smell. This is called **body odour (BO)**.

WORD BANK

Bacteria: single-celled organisms.
Organism: any living plant or animal, virus, bacterium, etc.

Simple steps for good personal hygiene

- **Wash daily** to remove stale sweat and bacteria that can cause odours.
- **Brush teeth twice a day** to prevent tooth decay and keep your breath from smelling.
- **Visit the dentist for regular checkups** and change your toothbrush on a regular basis.
- **Wash hands** after visiting the toilet and before each meal. This prevents the spread of bacteria.
- **Brush or comb your hair daily** to help remove dead skin cells and stimulate the flow of blood to the hair roots.
- **Wash your hair** on a regular basis, particularly if it is greasy.
- **Take care of your eyes** and visit the optician if you are having eye problems.
- **Take care of your feet** because you use them every day. Visit a chiropodist or doctor if you are experiencing foot problems.

CLOTHES CARE

Just as it is important to take care of your skin, it is important to take care of your clothes. Like the skin, clothing can contain many bacteria. Bacteria can thrive on clothing that has absorbed perspiration and spills. Clothing can also soak up odours, such as cooking odours and cigarette smoke. You may look good, but if your clothing does not look or smell good, all your efforts are wasted.

Clothing should be:

- washed on a regular basis
- ironed when necessary
- dried properly
- stored correctly.

It is important to know how to care for your clothing correctly. For this reason, a **care labelling system** is used to give instructions to ensure that clothing is laundered correctly. All garments have a care label

attached to them, similar to the one shown here. Washing machine instruction booklets also display these symbols.

This system gives instructions on how to wash, bleach, iron, dry clean and dry clothing. This system is used internationally, so any clothing that is imported into this country, or any clothing bought abroad, will use this same system to provide laundering instructions.

Washing symbols

The wash tub symbol is used to give instructions on how to wash clothing. There is a series of wash tub symbols for clothing made from different fibres. This symbol gives two types of information:

- the wash temperature: this is indicated below the water line
- the amount of washing machine **agitation:** this is indicated by a bar below the wash tub symbol, for example:

 No bar means normal machine action required

 Solid bar means reduced machine action required

 Broken bar means much reduced machine action required

	MAXIMUM WASH TEMPERATURE	WASH INSTRUCTIONS	SUITABLE FABRICS
[95]	Very hot 95°C	Maximum machine action. Rinse and spin.	White cotton and linen articles without special finishes.
[60]	Hot 60°C	Maximum machine action. Rinse and spin.	Cotton, linen or viscose articles, without special finishes where colours are fast at 60°C.
[50]	Hand hot 50°C	Medium machine action. Rinse with gradual cooling, reduced spin or drip dry.	Nylon, polyester cotton mixes, polyester cotton and viscose with special finishes, cotton and acrylic mixes.
[40]	Warm 40°C	Maximum machine action. Rinse and spin.	Cotton, linen or viscose articles where colours are fast at 40°C but not at 60°C.
[40]	Warm 40°C	Medium machine action. Rinse with gradual cooling, reduced spin or drip dry.	Acrylics, acetates and triacetate, including mixtures with wool, polyester and wool blends.
[40]	Warm 40°C	Minimum action, normal rinse and spin.	Wool, wool mixed with other fibres, silk.
[hand]	Hand wash only	Look at the garment label for further instructions.	
[cross]	Do not wash		

Bleaching symbols

Bleach is used to remove stains and soiling from clothing and fabrics.
Bleach is usually only used on white fabric.

Bleaching instructions are recognised by this triangle symbol.

This symbol indicates that the clothing or fabric can be bleached. The letters *Cl* indicate that chlorine bleach can be used.

A symbol with a cross through it means 'do not'. In this case the symbol means do **not** bleach.

Drying symbols

It is relatively easy to dry clothes. However, some items of clothing contain fibres that need to be dried in a particular way to make sure the fibres (and so the clothing) are not damaged.

Drying instructions are recognised by a square symbol.

This symbol means that clothing can be tumble-dried.

This symbol means that clothing should not be tumble-dried.

This symbol means that the clothing should be dried flat, that is, you should not hang this clothing on a washing line.

This symbol means that clothing can be line-dried, that is, you can hang this item on a washing line.

This symbol means that the clothing should be drip-dried, that is, it is better to hang the clothing when it is still wet.

Dry cleaning symbols

Some clothing cannot be cleaned in the normal way – using water and detergent. Some grease and stubborn stains are difficult to remove with water and detergent. In these cases, **dry cleaning** is used.

Dry cleaning instructions are recognised by a circle symbol.

The **A** means that the goods can be dry cleaned in **all** solvents.

The **P** and **F** mean that the goods can be dry cleaned using only certain specified solvents.

The solid line under this symbol means that extra care is needed during the dry cleaning process.

This symbol means do **not** dry clean.

The symbols A, F and P are for use by professional dry cleaners only. It is not necessary to know the specific dry cleaning solvents used.

Ironing symbols

Many items of clothing crease during washing and drying. Passing some dry or moist heat over the fibres of the clothing smoothes out any creases. It is important, however, to know how hot the iron should be. If it is too hot, the clothing may burn or melt, but if it is too cool, the clothing will remain creased.

 This symbol indicates how the clothing should be ironed. There are four iron symbols.

 A **hot** iron is required (210°C). Used for clothing made from cotton and linen.

 A **warm** iron is required (160°C). Used for clothing made from wool, silk, polyester mixes.

 A **cool** iron is required (120°C). Used for clothing made from nylon, polyester, acrylics, acetate, tricel and viscose.

 This symbol means that the clothing should **not** be ironed.

For you to do

1 Explain why an international care labelling system is important to the consumer.
2 What information does the care label below provide the consumer?

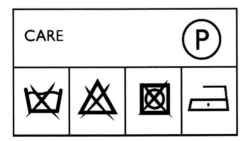

Care notes
- Some fabrics have special finishes (e.g. flame proof finishes). It is important to read carefully the care label on the garment for such items.
- The dyes used in some fabrics may start to run at certain temperatures. Where a label states **colourfast at 60°C** this means that the garment can be washed at this temperature without the dye running. You should read the care label instructions carefully for strongly coloured items.

HYGIENE IN RELATION TO FOOD HANDLING

Food hygiene is all about making sure that food is safe to eat. There are a number of rules that should be followed when preparing and cooking food to make sure it is safe to eat. These rules are listed below.

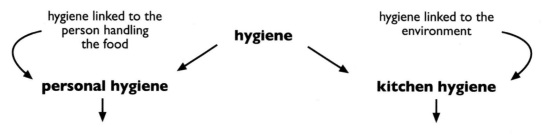

PERSONAL HYGIENE	KITCHEN HYGIENE
Jewellery must not be worn • Jewellery can be a breeding ground for bacteria. • Stones can fall out of jewellery and contaminate the food.	*All waste must be disposed of correctly* • This prevents spread of bacteria and the **infestation** of pests. • Waste bins should have well-fitting lids.
Cuts, spots, boils and skin infections are breeding grounds for bacteria • They should be covered with waterproof plasters. • The plasters should be coloured so they are visible if they fall off.	*Have separate washing facilities for hands and food* • This prevents the spread of bacteria. • Ideally have disposable cloths used for cleaning. • Separate cloths for hand drying and equipment drying.
Hands and nails must remain clean • Hands are in continual contact with food and can spread bacteria. • Nail varnish must be removed, as it may flake or chip into the food. • Hands should be washed on a regular basis, especially after visiting the toilet.	*Food preparation areas must be clean and well maintained* • Toilet facilities should be located well away from the food preparation area. • Surfaces should be easy to clean. • Lighting should allow for good visibility to make cleaning effective.
Hair must be tied back and covered completely • This prevents hair strands falling into food.	*Food should be covered at all times* • This prevents contamination with bacteria.
Clean protective clothing must be worn • This covers normal clothing and so prevents spread of bacteria. • Wear such clothing only in the food preparation and cooking area and wash it on a daily basis.	*A 'clean-as-you-go' approach should always be adopted* • Spills should be wiped up immediately – these not only attract bacteria, but can be a safety hazard. • All work surfaces should be cleaned before and after use. • All equipment should be cleaned after use.
Health issues must be considered • Coughing and sneezing associated with colds can spread bacteria to food. • Use disposable paper tissues and wash hands regularly. • Report all health problems to a supervisor.	*Animals must not be allowed in food preparation areas* • Animals are **carriers** of many bacteria and must be kept away from food preparation areas. • Report any infestation of pests (e.g. flies) to a supervisor/Environmental Health Officer.

The list on page 48 does not cover every single possible rule, but in your examination it is unlikely that you would be asked to provide more than six different hygiene measures. If you get a question in your exam to do with hygiene, read the question carefully to see if it specifies personal or kitchen hygiene. If it does not mention either, your answers can relate to either personal or kitchen hygiene.

The Foundation and General papers sometimes have illustrations of situations that are unhygienic. Remember to look for all the personal and kitchen hygiene rules, as well as remembering the points made in this section.

Internet activity

3 Visit the East Lindsey District Council website and click on the link to the hygiene poster rules.
Why would a company ask a member of staff to sign this notice/poster?

4 Visit the Foodlink website and complete the food safety quiz.

Links to these sites and other websites relating to Standard Grade Home Economics can be found at: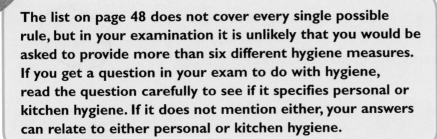

CAUSES, EFFECTS AND CONTROL OF FOOD SPOILAGE

Food spoilage is the process that leads to food changing in a way that makes it unfit for human consumption. Food spoilage is caused by the action of **enzymes** and **micro-organisms**.

Enzymes

Enzymes are chemicals that are found in food. These chemicals have important uses in food. They can cause food to deteriorate in three main ways:

- **ripening** – ripening of fruit and vegetables continues until the food becomes inedible (e.g. bananas become dark brown and very soft in texture)
- **browning** – enzymes can react with air causing the skin of certain foods, such as potatoes and apples, to discolour

- **oxidation** – enzymes can cause the loss of certain nutrients, such as vitamins A, C and B1, from food.

Micro-organisms

There are three main micro-organisms that you need to know about:

- bacteria
- moulds
- yeast.

Bacteria are single-celled organisms that are so small they cannot be seen by the naked eye. Not all bacteria are bad for us. We have useful bacteria in our intestines. Bacteria are also used in the manufacture of yoghurt and cheese. However, some bacteria can be harmful and it is these bacteria that can cause food to spoil and become dangerous to your health.

Bacteria can be dangerous in three main ways:

- the presence of some bacteria in our food can lead to **digestive upset**
- some bacteria produce **toxins** (poisons) which can lead to digestive upset
- some bacteria can produce **spores**, which in turn can produce poisons.

Moulds are a type of **fungus** that can cause food spoilage. Moulds produce spores, which can travel through the air. When they land on suitable food they begin to grow and multiply. Mould can be visible to the naked eye, such as moulds on bread. Certain types of moulds can produce poisons which will upset the digestive system. Not all moulds cause food spoilage. Moulds are used in some cheeses, such as Stilton, giving a characteristic colour and flavour.

Yeast is also a type of fungus. It is found in the air and soil as well as on the surface of some fruits. Yeast can cause food spoilage in certain types of foods, such as jams and meats. It causes food spoilage as it can affect the taste of food. Not all types of yeast are harmful. Yeast is used in the production of bread and wine.

Conditions for bacterial growth

All micro-organisms require certain conditions to survive and reproduce. These conditions are:

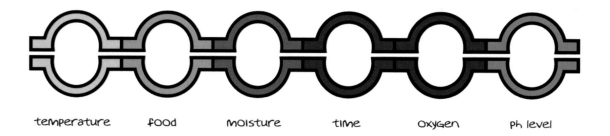

| temperature | food | moisture | time | oxygen | ph level |

When all of these conditions are present, they produce a chain of events that can lead to the growth and multiplication of bacteria. This in turn causes food spoilage and possible food poisoning.

WORD BANK

Spore: a special cell produced by bacteria that can withstand extreme conditions.

Germinate: to start to grow.

Dormant: something which is not active/not growing, but which has the ability to be active/grow later; like being asleep.

Temperature

Bacteria need warm conditions to grow and multiply. The ideal temperature zone for bacterial growth is between 30°C and 37°C. Some bacteria can still grow at temperatures between 10°C and 60°C. For this reason we often say that the **danger zone** for bacterial growth is between 5°C and 63°C. Most bacteria are destroyed at temperatures above 63°C.

However, some bacteria produce spores when conditions for growth become poor. Spores can survive for long periods of time until conditions for growth become ideal, when they can begin to **germinate** and produce new bacteria.

At temperatures below 5°C (the usual temperature of a domestic fridge) bacteria find it difficult to grow and multiply. At very cold temperatures, bacteria become **dormant** – they do not die, but they cannot grow or multiply.

Food

Bacteria require a source of food to grow and multiply. These foods usually contain large amounts of water and nutrients. Examples of suitable foods include:

- meat and meat products
- milk and dairy products
- fruit.

Moisture

Bacteria require moisture to grow and multiply. Bacteria cannot grow where there is no moisture. It is important to remember that both moulds and bacteria can produce spores, which can survive in dried foods, until such a time when they are **rehydrated** (have water added).

Time

Bacteria require time to grow and multiply. One bacterium can split into two every 20 minutes. In seven hours, the number of bacteria would reach several million. Foods which spoil very quickly in this way are called **perishable foods**.

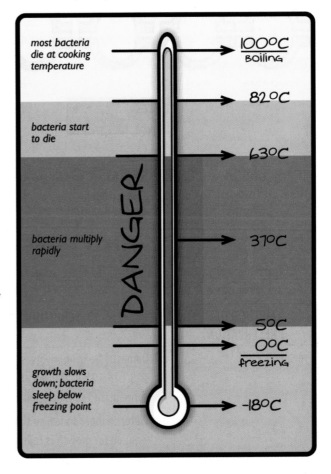

most bacteria die at cooking temperature — 100°C BOILING

— 82°C

bacteria start to die — 63°C

DANGER

bacteria multiply rapidly — 37°C

— 5°C
— 0°C freezing

growth slows down; bacteria sleep below freezing point — -18°C

Oxygen

Some bacteria require oxygen to grow and multiply. These bacteria are known as **aerobic bacteria**. Other bacteria grow best if there is no oxygen present. These are known as **anaerobic bacteria**.

pH

The **pH** of a substance is a measurement of how **acidic** or **alkaline** it is. A pH of 1 means the substance is very acidic. A pH of 14 means the substance is very alkaline. Most bacteria prefer pH conditions of between pH 6.6 and pH 7.5, that is, neither very alkaline nor very acidic (water has a pH of 7).

Moulds and yeast can survive at pH levels of 1–1.5. Food spoilage in these foods, such as fruits, is usually caused by yeast and moulds.

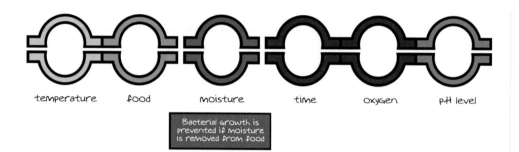

temperature   food   moisture   time   oxygen   pH level

Bacterial Growth is prevented if moisture is removed from food

If any one of the links in the food spoilage chain is broken, there is less chance of food being spoiled.

FOOD STORAGE AND PRESERVATION

Conditions which cause food to spoil due to bacterial growth can be controlled in order to **preserve** food.

METHOD OF PRESERVATION	DESCRIPTION AND COMMENTS	SUITABLE FOODS
Freezing	• Domestic freezing involves the use of temperatures of −18°C to −22°C. This very cold temperature makes bacteria dormant and so food spoilage is reduced. • Water changes to ice, so the amount of available moisture required for growth is reduced. • Some fruits and vegetables are blanched (dipped in boiling water) before freezing. This destroys the enzymes that can make food spoil. • Note: once food is defrosted, bacterial growth will increase.	Meat, chicken, fish, vegetables. Most foods can be frozen for periods of up to 18 months. Foods with a very high water content are not suitable for freezing. Dairy products tend not to freeze well.
Chilling	• Food is stored at a temperature above freezing – usually between 0°C and 4°C. This low temperature slows down the rate of bacterial multiplication and spoilage is also slowed down but not stopped. • Moulds can still grow in cold temperatures.	Chilled ready-to-eat foods, salad items, dairy produce, meat, fish.
Jam/marmalade making	• The initial boiling of the fruit will destroy enzymes, preventing later spoilage. • The initial boiling of the fruit will destroy micro-organisms (but not spores), preventing later spoilage. • The high concentration of sugar added during the jam-making process reduces bacterial growth due to its dehydrating effect. • Jam bottles are normally heated before jam is added. This process destroys micro-organisms found in the jars.	Most berry fruits, black and red currants, plums, apricots, oranges, grapefruit.

METHOD OF PRESERVATION	DESCRIPTION AND COMMENTS	SUITABLE FOODS
Pickling/chutney making	• The initial boiling of the ingredients will destroy enzymes, preventing later spoilage. • The initial boiling of the ingredients will destroy micro-organisms (but not spores), preventing later spoilage • The high concentration of acid (vinegar) prevents bacterial growth and multiplication. • The pickle/chutney bottles are normally heated before the product is added. This process destroys micro-organisms found in the bottles.	Many fruits and vegetables can be used to make pickles and chutney. Some fish (e.g. herring) can be pickled.
Vacuum packaging	• Normally used in conjunction with chilling. • Oxygen is removed and so micro-organisms cannot multiply unless they are anaerobic. Sometimes chemical preservatives are added to keep them longer. • Another form of vacuum packaging is Modified Atmosphere Packaging. The gas content within the packaging material is altered, that is, the amount of oxygen is reduced and the amount of carbon dioxide is increased. This slows down the rate of food spoilage and aerobic bacteria cannot grow.	Cold meats, cheese, bacon, fish. Bacon and ready-prepared washed salads and salad leaves.

HINTS & TIPS

There are many other techniques of food preservation such as salting, smoking, bottling and canning. You will not be asked a specific question about these methods in an examination.

For you to do

5 Next time you are in a supermarket look at the variety of jams and marmalades that are available. Make a list of all the different types that you can buy. Alternatively, visit the website of a major supermarket to undertake this activity.

6 Find out what each of the following terms mean:
   a freezer burn
   b quick-freeze
   c Tetra Pak.

FOOD POISONING

Food poisoning is an illness caused by the eating of contaminated or poisonous food.

Causes

Food poisoning is usually caused by **bacterial contamination** of food, that is, the food becomes contaminated with bacteria which then enter the digestive system and cause illness. Food infected with bacteria may look, smell and taste normal, so it can be difficult to tell if a food may cause food poisoning. The types of bacteria that can cause illness are known as **pathogenic bacteria**.

Bacteria are generally only harmful if they are present in very large numbers in food. Some food may have been infected with bacteria for a long period of time and toxins (poisons) may have formed in the food before consumption. Other bacteria only produce the toxins once they have entered the digestive system.

Symptoms of food poisoning

Food poisoning can be mild or severe. The symptoms will vary slightly, depending on what type of bacteria is responsible for the poisoning. General symptoms include:

- severe vomiting
- diarrhoea
- exhaustion
- headache
- fever
- abdominal pain
- tiredness.

If you think you have food poisoning you should seek medical attention. You should also avoid preparing or handling food, in case you transfer food poisoning bacteria on to other people.

PREVENTING FOOD SPOILAGE, CONTAMINATION AND POISONING

There are a large number of steps that we can take to prevent food spoilage, food contamination and so food poisoning. These start when we buy food and finish when we serve food.

Buying foods

STEP TO TAKE	REASON
Do not buy food that has passed its 'use by date'.	The food is perishable and may be contaminated with bacteria. It is illegal to sell food once it has reached its use by date.
Do not buy tinned food which is bashed, blown or rusted.	This means that the food has not been stored correctly and has potentially been contaminated.
Do not buy frozen food (e.g. vegetables) which have frozen together in the pack.	This indicates that the food has started to defrost at some stage, so bacteria may have grown in this time. If the food has been refrozen, this means more dormant bacteria.
Ensure that packaging is intact.	Damaged packaging may allow food to become contaminated.
Buy only from shops that are clean and hygienic.	Use your common sense. A shop that sells food and which looks unclean may not be the best place to buy from. Make sure the shop assistants observe good hygiene.

Transporting food back to the home

Just as it is important to use your common sense when buying food, it is important to remember to use your common sense when packing food to prevent food contamination.

STEP TO TAKE	REASON
Plan your shopping journey in advance.	Buy frozen foods last, and only when you are ready to go home. You do not want to give the food time to start to defrost as bacteria may start to multiply.
Try to keep frozen and chilled foods cold.	Pack in the boot of the car – which may be the coldest part of the car. Use cool boxes where possible to keep food cold. Pack frozen and chilled foods together to maintain cold conditions.
Keep cooked and uncooked foods apart.	Bacteria may spread from uncooked to cooked foods, so keep them apart when packing the shopping.
Pack dry and moist foods separately.	This will prevent dry food products, or their packaging, from becoming damp.
Pack household chemicals away from food.	This will prevent any chemical contamination of food and prevent chemical odours tainting food.

Storing food in the home

Correct storage of food in the home is essential if food contamination is to be prevented. There are many simple rules that should be followed to ensure that food stays fresh for as long as possible.

STEP TO TAKE	REASON
Unpack food as quickly as possible – especially perishable foods.	Perishable and frozen foods should be placed into chilled conditions as quickly as possible to ensure that bacterial growth is not assisted.
Use up old stocks of food before buying new ones.	This ensures that food does not reach its expiry date. Throw out food that is out of date – the quality of the food cannot be guaranteed.
Keep dry food in cool, dry, clean places.	This ensures that food remains in good condition and prevents contamination from other sources.

Some tips for special foods

Eggs
Store eggs in the refrigerator to keep them fresh. Store them in the box with the pointed end down – this keeps the yolks positioned in the centre of the egg.

Canned foods
Once opened treat the contents as fresh, so empty any unused contents into a bowl, cover, refrigerate and use within 2 days or as specified on the label. Never use damaged cans.

Foods in the store cupboard
Foods in the store cupboard (e.g. tins and packets), should be rotated, that is, use up old stock first and never put a new supply of food on top of an older item.

Barbecues
When barbecuing – particularly raw poultry, meat and fish – it is important not to have the barbecue too hot, otherwise the outside of the food becomes overcooked, whilst the inside remains undercooked. It is very important to use separate utensils for handling raw and cooked foods.

Common food poisoning situations

Frozen items, for example, frozen turkey, need to be defrosted fully before cooking. If not, the centre of the food does not cook to a high enough temperature to kill pathogenic (disease-producing) bacteria present, but it will be warm enough for bacteria to grow and multiply. Your Christmas present from the bacteria will be food poisoning!

Foods that are **cooked in advance** to be used later should be covered and kept in a refrigerator until needed. This will keep the food safe from pests such as flies. It will also reduce the amount of time the food will spend in the danger zone of 5°C – 63°C, so there will be less time for bacteria to grow and multiply if the food has been contaminated.

It is very important that the food is **reheated** to at least a core temperature of 82°C to destroy bacteria. Food should never be reheated on more than one occasion.

Cooked rice can be very dangerous if it has not been cooled quickly and then reheated to the correct temperature. Rice contains a bacterium that can produce spores and toxins. It is better if rice is cooked as and when needed.

Cross-contamination of food

We have seen that bacteria can contaminate food. The main carriers of contamination – and causes of **cross-contamination** – are:

- humans
- pets and other animals
- rubbish
- food.

Humans

Bacteria are found on our bodies – our hair, hands, mouth, nose, ears, and intestines all contain bacteria. When we sneeze, cough, spit and blow our nose, we are spreading bacteria. Care must be taken when working with food.

Pets and other animals

Pets and other animals such as flies, mice and rats are all carriers of bacteria – some of which are pathogenic. Animals should be kept out of food preparation areas.

Rubbish

Rubbish attracts all types of animals – from flies to stray cats and dogs. If rubbish is stored in or near food preparation areas, the risk of bacterial contamination of food is increased. Rubbish also contains lots of bacteria, which can be spread to food.

Food

Raw food may come into the home contaminated with bacteria. If stored correctly and cooked correctly, this should not cause problems. By following simple rules, cross-contamination can be prevented.

WORD BANK

Cross-contamination: the process by which bacteria are transferred from one area to another. All of the carriers listed are potential vehicles for cross-contamination. This is a major cause of food contamination and food poisoning.

RULE	REASON
Always store cooked and raw foods apart.	To prevent bacteria from spreading from the raw food to the cooked food.
Use separate equipment for raw foods and cooked foods – or wash thoroughly before use.	To prevent bacteria from spreading from the raw food to the equipment being used. If not cleaned properly, cross-contamination occurs.
Wash all work surfaces thoroughly after preparing raw foods.	This will eliminate the risk of cross-contamination, particularly if you use hot water and a detergent.
Wash hands thoroughly after handling raw foods.	This will eliminate the risk of cross-contamination, particularly if you use hot water and a detergent.
Do not use wooden chopping boards, wooden spoons or cracked crockery if possible.	Wooden chopping boards, wooden spoons and cracked crockery may all harbour bacteria.
Disinfect cleaning cloths regularly. Ideally, use disposable cloths.	To prevent bacteria crossing over to the cloth (and then contaminating other areas) after wiping a chopping board after cutting raw meat.
Cover food at all stages of production.	This prevents cross-contamination from animals such as flies or from air-borne particles and organisms.

Important food safety temperatures

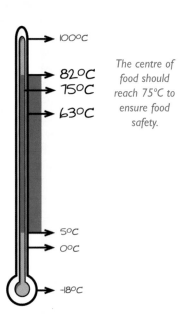

Reheat food to a core temperature of at least 82°C to destroy bacteria. Food should never be reheated more than once.

Foods that have been cooked and are to be sold (e.g. in a café) have to be held at a temperature of at least 63°C

100°C

82°C
75°C
63°C

The centre of food should reach 75°C to ensure food safety.

5°C
0°C

-18°C

Food labelling and food hygiene

Specific labelling requirements help prevent poor food storage and so prevent food spoilage and food poisoning.

Date marking

USE BY
8 OCTOBER

We already know that we cannot always tell if food is 'off' simply by looking at and smelling the food. For this reason, a **Use By** date mark on food is important. The Use By date is found on products that are **highly perishable**, such as meat products, cream, yoghurts and ready meals. This means that the food **must be used by the date given**. If the food is consumed after this date, health can be put at risk. These products are usually high-risk foods, which are foods that provide ideal growing conditions for bacteria. It is against the law for a retailer to sell or display food for sale which has gone past its Use By date. It is important to remember that the Use By date only applies to the condition of the food when purchased, so freezing or cooking food after purchase extends its life.

The **Best Before** date is found on products that are less perishable. This label means that the product is at its best (in terms of quality, flavour and texture) before the date shown. The food may still be consumed after this date, but it may not be at its best quality.

BEST BEFORE
13 JULY 2008

Food manufacturers also provide other information that can be very useful in trying to prevent food spoilage and food poisoning.

Food labels have to provide instructions for safe storage. These are important as the Use By and Best Before dates are based on the consumer storing the product correctly.

STORAGE INSTRUCTIONS	STORAGE INSTRUCTIONS	STORAGE INSTRUCTIONS
Keep refrigerated. Do not freeze.	Store in a cool dry place.	Store in a cool dry place. Use within 6 months of opening and before the Best Before Date.

Instructions found on a tub of yoghurt   *Instructions found on a carton of hot chocolate powder*   *Instructions found on a glass jar of curry paste*

Manufacturers also have to provide directions to ensure the safe preparation or cooking of the food. If food has to be cooked, then accurate instructions have to be given to ensure that the food can be cooked correctly and so prevent food poisoning.

BEST COOKED FROM FROZEN
Place in a pre-heated oven at 200°C, Gas mark 6 for 1 hour and 10 minutes. *Ensure product is piping hot before serving.*

Instructions for cooking a pre-prepared chicken pie.

Chilled and frozen foods

We often buy frozen food and it is important that we store it correctly to prevent food spoilage. Food labels also provide guidance to help consumers store these foods correctly.

Pre-frozen food can be stored in the icebox of a refrigerator or in a domestic freezer. To help the consumer know how long they can safely store food in a refrigerator, all have a **star rating** – usually found on the door of the icebox. This star rating system tells you how long you can store pre-frozen foods.

 This means that pre-frozen food can be safely stored for a maximum of one week.

 This means that pre-frozen food can be safely stored for a maximum of one month.

 This means that pre-frozen food can be safely stored for a maximum of three months.

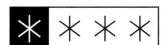 This means that pre-frozen foods and fresh foods can be stored in iceboxes for a maximum of three months.

 You cannot use the icebox of a refrigerator to store non-frozen food. The temperature of the icebox does not reach a sufficiently low temperature to cause bacteria to become dormant.

For you to do

7 Complete the following wordsearch which is all about food safety.

- A symptom of food poisoning
- The date mark used for perishable foods
- The temperature which reheated food should reach to thaw out food
- The number of months that you can store pre-frozen food in a three-star refrigerator icebox
- The term used for the transporter of bacteria from one place to another
- The person you should report to if you think you have food poisoning
- To thaw food

d	e	f	r	o	s	y	g	e	e	e	e
e	i	g	t	e	d	d	n	i	i	i	t
d	t	d	w	i	e	o	i	g	g	g	h
e	e	y	o	e	f	c	t	h	h	h	e
f	d	f	u	d	r	t	i	t	t	r	i
r	o	e	r	s	o	o	m	y	y	d	g
s	c	t	t	o	e	r	o	t	t	o	h
v	e	h	e	h	s	b	v	w	w	v	t
t	h	r	e	e	g	t	y	o	s	d	y
v	v	y	c	a	r	r	i	e	r	e	t
o	e	i	g	h	i	d	e	f	i	v	e
e	i	g	h	t	y	r	d	e	f	r	c

REFRIGERATORS AND FREEZERS

Refrigerators and freezers play an important role in the prevention of food spoilage and food poisoning. In both refrigerators and freezers, temperature is reduced and so bacterial growth is reduced. However, they must both be used correctly in order to prevent food spoilage and food poisoning.

Use of refrigerators

A refrigerator normally has an internal temperature of **between 2°C and 4°C**. This is sufficiently cold to reduce bacterial growth, but not stop it. For this reason, refrigeration is only a short-term storage measure. Some refrigerators have an icebox. This is the coldest part of the fridge, and is normally marked with a star rating. There are, however, a number of important rules that should be followed to ensure the food is stored safely in the refrigerator.

For you to do

8 Record the temperature of the refrigerator in your home. What was the recorded temperature? What can you conclude from this simple test?

Use of freezers

A freezer normally has an internal temperature of **–18°C or below**. This is cold enough to stop bacterial growth. For this reason, freezing food is suitable for both short and longer term food storage.

Some freezers have a quick-freeze facility where the internal temperature of the freezer can be reduced to –24°C.

Most food contain large amounts of water. When water is frozen, ice is formed. Large ice crystals are formed when food is frozen slowly. This can damage the cell structure of the food. When the food defrosts, the water enclosed within the cells is released. The food can appear to look 'soggy'.

RULE	COMMENT
Ensure the refrigerator is working at a temperature between 2°C and 4°C.	Use a refrigerator thermometer to ensure that the interior of the refrigerator is working in this temperature range. Do not place hot food in the interior of the refrigerator – cool it first. (Placing hot food in the refrigerator will increase the temperature above 4°C and bacterial growth will increase.) Do not leave the refrigerator door open for long periods of time as this will allow the temperature of the fridge to rise to more than 4°C.
Do not overload the refrigerator.	Cold air needs to circulate around the food which is stored inside the fridge. This cannot happen if the refrigerator is overfilled.
Store food correctly in the refrigerator.	To prevent cross-contamination, raw and cooked foods should be stored separately, with raw food stored below cooked food. All food should be covered, not only to prevent cross-contamination but also to prevent moisture loss. Remove any food from the refrigerator when it has reached its date mark.
Regular maintenance of the refrigerator is important.	Keep the interior of the refrigerator clean, removing spills and food deposits whenever they occur. This will help prevent contamination of food. If the refrigerator needs to be defrosted, this should be done regularly, to prevent a build-up of ice on the icebox.

At lower temperatures, smaller ice crystals form so the damage to the cell structure is reduced. Therefore, when the food is defrosted, it keeps its shape better.

There are, however, a number of important rules that should be followed to ensure the food is stored safely in the freezer.

RULE	COMMENT
Ensure the freezer is working at a temperature below −18ºC.	Use a freezer thermometer to ensure that the interior of the freezer is working at this temperature. Do not place hot food in the interior of the freezer – cool it first. (Placing hot food in the freezer will increase the temperature and bacterial growth will increase.) Do not leave the freezer door open for long periods of time, as this will allow the temperature of the freezer to rise – particularly if the freezer is an upright freezer.
Do not overload the freezer.	Cold air needs to circulate around the food which is stored inside the freezer. This cannot happen if the freezer is overfilled.
Store food correctly in the freezer.	All food should be clearly marked showing its contents and date when frozen. This will allow you to take out the food you require, encourage you to use food in a timely fashion, and allow you to throw out food that has been stored for too long. Wrap food well before freezing – otherwise the food will dry out. Only freeze food which is in its best condition – it will last for a longer period of time. Remove as much air from the food packaging as possible before freezing. This will help prevent the food drying out during storage.
Regular maintenance of the freezer is important.	Keep the interior of the freezer clean, removing spills and food deposits whenever they occur. This will help prevent contamination of food. Defrost the freezer regularly.
Never refreeze defrosted food.	When the food is thawing, bacterial growth will increase. When you refreeze the food, you are freezing food with an increased number of bacteria present.

Quick Quiz

1 You are reheating a vegetable pie. What temperature should the pie reach to ensure food safety?
2 You are checking the temperature of your refrigerator. What is the maximum temperature allowed to ensure food safety?
3 What does the following storage information, found on a refrigerator, tell you? ✳ ✳ ✳
4 At what temperature do most bacteria start to die?
5 At what temperature does a domestic freezer work?
6 What are the symptoms of food poisoning?
7 On what types of food would you find a 'Use By' date?
8 Where in a domestic fridge would you store pre-cooked foods?
9 What is the difference between personal and kitchen hygiene?

CHAPTER 5: SAFE WORKING PRACTICES

In this chapter
- Safe working practices
- Use of food preparation equipment
- Care of clothing
- Sewing equipment
- Home safety

SAFE WORKING PRACTICES

Every year, hundreds of people are killed or injured in the home as a result of accidents. Many of these accidents can be avoided by taking simple preventative measures. The main accidents that occur in the home are:

- cuts
- **burns**
- **scalds**

- falls
- electric shocks
- poisonings.

Young children and elderly people are the two groups who are most at risk from accidents in the home. Young children tend to be curious and this can lead to accidents. Elderly people may become less able to react to situations as they happen and this can lead to accidents. This section is all about trying to prevent accidents before they occur.

USE OF FOOD PREPARATION EQUIPMENT

In the kitchen, we use a lot of food preparation equipment that can be dangerous if not used correctly.

Care must be taken when using **hot fat**, **oil** and **liquids**. These cooking media are potentially dangerous because:

- they can reach a very high temperature
- when spilt they can cover a large section of the body very easily.

When cooking with hot fats and oils, a **thermostatically controlled** frying pan is the best option, as the pan will automatically cut off when the correct temperature has been reached. A pan of hot oil or fat must never be left unattended as it can quickly catch fire.

Burn: skin damage caused by dry heat, for example, match or hot pan.
Scald: skin damage caused by wet heat, for example, steam or boiling water.
Arc: a powerful flow of electricity which goes across a space between two points, for example, sparking.
Thermostatic control: a device on an appliance that regulates the operating temperature.

FOOD PREPARATION EQUIPMENT	PROCEDURES FOR SAFE USE
Sharp utensils (e.g. knives)	• Sharp knives, scissors and skewers are a potential danger because of their sharp edges. They should never be left lying on a work surface in case young children can reach them. • Knives should be kept in a knife block or in a drawer that can be locked. • Scissors and skewers should be kept in an area children cannot access. • Sharp utensils which have been used for food preparation should be placed in a safe area until they are ready to be cleaned. Leaving such objects in the sink can be dangerous.
Gas and electric cookers	• Gas appliances should always be fitted by a registered gas fitter. • If a gas leak is suspected, contact TRANSCO immediately. (TRANSCO is the body responsible for the delivery of gas to the home.) • Cookers should not be placed next to windows if there is a danger of gas burners being blown out by draughts or if there are blinds or curtains nearby that might catch fire. • Switch off cookers when not being used. • Use oven gloves when taking items from the oven. • Use a hob guard to prevent young children gaining access to the hob area of the cooker and pulling hot pans from the hob. • Do not allow young children into the kitchen without supervision when the cooker is operating.
Electrical equipment	• Never handle electrical equipment with wet hands – this can lead to electrocution. • Always switch off electrical equipment at the mains supply before and after use. • Never assemble or disassemble electrical equipment, such as food processors, when plugged into the electricity supply. • Never immerse electrical equipment in water or put it in a dishwasher. • Never use electrical equipment that is damaged in any way. This includes frayed flexes and damaged plugs. • Always check that the fuse used in the plug is the correct ampage for the appliance. • Always read instruction manuals before use.
Microwave oven	• The use of a microwave oven to fry food is not recommended as there is no way to regulate the temperature of the fat/oil. • Microwave cookers should be tested yearly for possible microwave leakage. • Do not place metal objects in microwave ovens. This can lead to **arcing** (sparking) which can damage the oven. • When using clingfilm on products which are to be cooked in the microwave, use the non-PVC type which is safe for use in microwave ovens. • Microwave containers can get very hot – remove them from the oven carefully and remove any lid or clingfilm covering the food with great care.

If a fat or oil fire occurs

- **Do not panic.** Keep calm.
- **Switch off** the gas burner or electric cooker ring.
- Place a **damp cloth** or **fire blanket** over the burning pan.
- Leave the pan to **cool down**.
- **NEVER grab the pan and try to take it outside**. The flames may blow on to your body. The oxygen in the air will feed the fire and again put you at further risk.
- **NEVER throw water over the fire.** This will cause the hot fat to spit and increase the force of the fire.

CARE OF CLOTHING

When caring for clothing it is important that we follow safe practices when using items of equipment.

LAUNDERING EQUIPMENT	PROCEDURES FOR SAFE USE
Washing machine	• Follow the general instructions listed on page 63 for the use of electrical equipment. Read the manufacturer's instructions before use. • Do not leave detergents and other chemicals lying where young children have access to them. • Ensure that any safety lock features on the washing machine are working. • Ensure that young children do not have access to the washing machine while it is being used – some wash programmes use very hot water.
Tumble-drier	• Follow the general instructions listed on page 63 for the use of electrical equipment. Read the manufacturer's instructions before use. • Ensure that any safety lock features on the tumble-drier are working. • Ensure that young children do not have access to the tumble-drier while it is being used.
Iron	• Follow the general instructions listed on page 63 for the use of electrical equipment. Read the manufacturer's instructions before use. • Always set the iron to the correct temperature for the type of fabric to be ironed. • Never leave an iron unattended – especially if young children are in the home. • If using a steam iron, add water only when the appliance is switched off. • Rest the iron on its heel between ironing garments. Resting the iron on its sole plate can be dangerous. • Leave the iron to cool down in a safe place (out of the reach of children) before storing the iron away.

LAUNDERING EQUIPMENT	PROCEDURES FOR SAFE USE
Ironing board	• Use an ironing board that is level and steady when being used. This will prevent the iron from slipping or toppling off the ironing board. • Store in a safe and secure place where it cannot topple over and cause an accident. • Make sure that the ironing board cover is firmly secured with no loose ties that can attract a child's attention. • Never leave an ironing board unattended when there are young children about.

SEWING EQUIPMENT

When using sewing equipment there are a number of safety precautions that have to be considered.

SEWING EQUIPMENT	PROCEDURES FOR SAFE USE
Pins and needles	• Pick up immediately any pins or needles that are dropped on the ground. If left on the floor, they may cause an accident to the foot or children may pick up and swallow them or otherwise injure themselves. • Store pins and needles in a safe container away from the reach of young children. • Pins and needles are dangerous. Never place them in the mouth or use them for play.
Scissors	• Scissors can pose potential danger because of their sharp edges and pointed ends. Never leave them lying on a work surface in case young children can reach them. • Keep scissors in a drawer that can be locked. • When carrying scissors, hold them by the closed blades with the handle uppermost. • When passing scissors to someone else, hold the closed blades in your hand and pass on to the other person with the handles uppermost.
Sewing machine	• Follow the general instructions listed on page 63 for the use of electrical equipment. Read the instruction manual before using the sewing machine. • Only one person at a time should operate the sewing machine – it is very easy to lose your concentration and this can be dangerous. • Keep hands and loose clothing well away from the moving needle. • Pack the sewing machine away after use and store it in an area where young children have no access. When packing the sewing machine away, ensure that the needle is at its lowest position – this prevents any accidents when unpacking. • Take care when lifting a sewing machine – it is heavy and can cause back strain if lifted awkwardly. • Maintain the sewing machine regularly, to ensure it works correctly and safely.

HOME SAFETY

All of the safe practices listed on pages 63–65 will help prevent accidents and ensure that the home is a safe place. There are many more safety precautions that can be taken throughout the home. Most of these are common-sense measures. No matter how safe you try to make your home, some accidents are still likely to happen.

HINTS & TIPS

In an examination you would generally be asked to identify the main causes of accidents in the home and then describe measures that you would take to prevent such accidents happening. The table below describes some common hazards and accidents which occur in the home (and which frequently feature in exam questions) and suggests how the accidents could be prevented.

HAZARD	TYPE OF ACCIDENT	PRECAUTION
Sharp objects (e.g. scissors, knives, pins) lying on work areas	Cut	Remove item to a safe area out of the reach of children. Remove to a locked drawer/cupboard.
Broken glass/crockery on the floor or on a worktop	Cut	Remove item from the area, wrap in lots of newspaper and dispose of safely.
Open coal-fire in a room	Burn	Do not light the fire unless there is adult supervision in the room. Place a fireguard round an open fire to prevent access to the fire by young children and to prevent sparks landing on carpets.
Matches/lighter left lying on a work area	Burn	Store matches/lighter in an area where young children cannot gain access.
Naked flames and heat-generating equipment in the kitchen	Burn	Do not let young children into the kitchen unless supervised.
Mirror, banners, pictures over a fireplace	Burn	Do not place items which will be of interest to young children over or near the fireplace.
Fireworks/other flammable materials left lying in a garden/cupboard	Burn	Move to an area where children do not have access, preferably in a locked drawer or cupboard.
Removing foods from an oven using a teacloth/towel	Burn	Use oven gloves which are designed to provide an insulating layer between the hands and the hot dish.
Saucepans on the cooker hob with pan handles sticking out	Scald	Turn the pan handles to the back or the sides of the cooker hob. Never allow children in the kitchen unsupervised. Use a cooker guard on the hob to prevent pans being toppled over.
Hot drinks, teapots lying on tables/work area	Scald	Do not leave hot drinks on tables, especially tables with tablecloths. A young child could pull the tablecloth and the hot drinks off the table.

HAZARD	TYPE OF ACCIDENT	PRECAUTION
Stairway/hall dimly lit	Fall	Ensure that stairways and other dimly lit areas have sufficient lighting to ensure good visibility.
Objects (e.g. toys, books, trailing flex) left lying on floor	Fall	Tidy away all objects after use. Shorten flex lengths to prevent them trailing.
Rug placed on a polished floor	Fall	Do not place a rug on a highly polished floor unless it can be firmly secured in place.
Spills on the floor	Fall	Wipe up all spills immediately – especially if on a floor surface that could become slippery.
Babies/young children climbing stairs/ entering the kitchen	Fall	Safety gates should be used to prevent babies and young children entering areas that can be dangerous.
Person using a stool to reach a high cupboard	Fall	Step-ladders should be used to reach high areas as chairs and tables may collapse under the weight of a person. They may also be wobbly.
Using electrical equipment with wet hands	Electric shock	Only use electrical equipment with dry hands. Do not operate on/off switches with wet hands. Do not operate electrical equipment in the bathroom.
Overloaded power switches/adapters	Electric shock	Never overload power sockets.
Frayed flex on electrical equipment	Electric shock	Frayed flexes must always be repaired/replaced. Do not use the appliance until repaired.
Child sticking fingers into electric socket	Electric shock	Use electric socket guards when there are young children in the house.
Medicines, chemicals, alcohol, etc., left lying on work areas	Poisoning	All medicines should be kept in a special cabinet out of the reach of young children. Chemicals and alcohol should be kept in areas which children cannot access.
Cleaning fluids kept in lemonade bottles	Poisoning	Always label chemicals clearly. Chemicals should be kept in areas which children cannot access.

Safety facts

- Every year in the UK, about 26,000 children under the age of 5 are burnt or scalded in the home.
- A hot drink is capable of scalding a small child up to 15 minutes after it is made.
- Boys have more accidents than girls.
- Approximately 1500 people aged over 75 die annually as the result of a fall.

And did you know:

- in 2003, 2000 people attended hospital after being bitten by a rat
- four people needed treatment after accidental suffocation and strangulation while in bed
- three people required medical attention after being bitten or struck by a crocodile or alligator.

For you to do

I   Study the illustration below. List all the safety hazards in the picture, then describe what should be done to prevent an accident happening.

Internet activity

I   Visit the Glasgow City Council website and answer these questions.

a   How many people in Glasgow are admitted to hospital each year as a result of accidents in the home?

b   List two functions of the Home Safety Officer.

c   If you were an elderly person and wanted some home safety advice, who would be the best person to contact?

d   Try to find out similar information for your own area.

2   Visit the Home Safety Game website. Click on the Play Game icon and see how quickly you can spot all the dangers. Make a note of your time. Try again and see if you can spot all the dangers in less time.

Links to this site and other websites relating to Standard Grade Home Economics can be found at: LECKIE&LECKIE Learning Lab

Quick Quiz

Select the correct answer **a**, **b**, **c** or **d** for each of the questions below.

1 Where shouldn't you store knives?

    a Knife block   **b** Locked drawer

    c Work surface   **d** Knife rack

2 Which organisation should you contact if you think you have a gas leak?

    a BBC   **b** TRANSCO

    c CORGI   **d** TUC

3 What action should you take if you have a chip pan fire?

    a Panic   **b** Take the pan outdoors

    c Turn off the electricity/gas source   **d** Throw water over it to put it out

4 When cooking food in a microwave which of the following should not be used? You can select more than one.

    a PVC clingfilm   **b** Non-PVC clingfilm

    c Aluminium foil   **d** Glass dish

5 What should you do when passing scissors to another person?

    a Throw them to the person   **b** Pass to the person, handle first

    c Pass to the person, blades first   **d** Tell them to get their own pair

6 What causes a scald?

    a Dry heat   **b** Wet heat

    c Both wet and dry heat   **d** A knife

7 What item should you use for removing hot food from an oven?

    a Dry dish towel   **b** Wet dish towel

    c Oven gloves   **d** Fish slice

8 Which of the following groups are prone to accidents?

    a The elderly and young children   **b** The elderly and teenagers

    c Teenagers and young children   **d** Young children and adults

9 Why should you have your microwave oven tested every year?

    a To make sure it is not leaking   **b** To make sure it is working

    c To make sure it is clean   **d** To provide employment to people

10 What is a safety gate?

    a A safety device to prevent children entering rooms where there is a potential danger

    b A gate to prevent burglars getting into your house

    c A gate placed on your cooker hob to prevent pans toppling over

    d A device placed in front of a fire

CHAPTER 6: DESIGN FEATURES

In this chapter
- Influences on choice of materials and resources
- Design and design features
- Conservation of resources

INFLUENCES ON CHOICE OF MATERIALS AND RESOURCES

There are a number of important considerations that we have to think about before buying goods and services. We all have different ideas about things that we like and dislike; we all have our favourite colours and our favourite foods. We take these into consideration when we buy goods and services.

What do we mean by materials and equipment?

Materials
- food
- clothing
- footwear

Equipment
- food preparation
- basic sewing
- **white goods**

Whatever the choice of item, there are a number of factors that will be considered before purchase.

White goods: large items of electrical equipment such as cookers, washing machines and tumble-driers.

Income	More income – generally means greater choice of items	
	Less income – generally means more restricted choice of items	
Size	If you wear size 4 shoes, then you are limited to what is available in your size	
	If you are buying a cooker and it needs to fit into a particular space in the kitchen then you are limited to what is available to fit that space	
Location	Urban	There may be greater choice of shops and stores and so choice is increased
		Also have access to mail order, internet and TV shopping channels
	Rural	There may be a more limited choice of shops and stores which in turn limits choice
		Shopping using mail order, TV channels and internet may have to be considered
Advertising	Often targeted at particular groups and can be designed to make you feel that you need this product	*Can lead to the purchase of items that you really did not need (called impulse buying)*
Payment facilities	Cash only	Credit available
	Interest-free credit	*May make payment easier or more*
What you have already	Will determine what you want to buy	*May be bought to match an existing item (e.g. colour)*

DESIGN AND DESIGN FEATURES

Whenever you decide to buy a particular product, there may be a wide selection available to you, even if you have limited funds.

In such cases, you will have to look at the types of **design features** available on each of the different products, and then decide which of these are the most important to you. Some of the design features of a backpack are shown below.

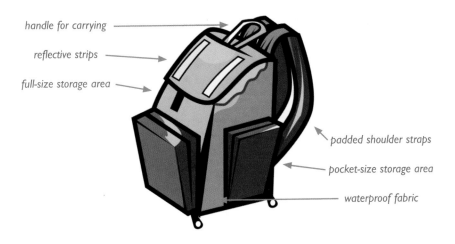

handle for carrying

reflective strips

full-size storage area

padded shoulder straps

pocket-size storage area

waterproof fabric

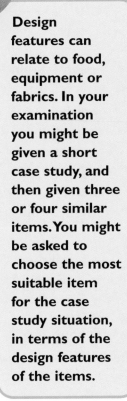

Design features can relate to food, equipment or fabrics. In your examination you might be given a short case study, and then given three or four similar items. You might be asked to choose the most suitable item for the case study situation, in terms of the design features of the items.

If you are looking for a backpack and want it to be brightly coloured, this one might not be the best choice for you. You would then need to look at other types and designs until you found the one that meets all your needs and wishes. As you go through this process, you are looking at and considering all the design features that will make the backpack suitable for you.

For you to do

1 Have you ever bought an item of clothing or an accessory and then asked yourself whether you really needed or wanted it? Describe one situation and explain what made you buy this item.

2 A 14 year old teenager is planning to buy a new sports shirt. The sports shirt needs to be blue in colour and cost less than £50.00. The shirt should be short-sleeved. Using the internet, or other resources available, find a suitable sports shirt for a teenage boy or girl. Take a photocopy or printout of the sports shirt and explain your choice in terms of design features.

Designing for a purpose

When a designer is designing a product, he or she will have to think not only about the design features, but also about what the item is going to be used for, that is, he or she will have to design the item to make sure that it is **fit for its purpose**. When thinking about the design of an item, there are a number of different **areas** that a designer will have to think about:

- **Materials** to be used – are they suitable for the item?
- **Construction** – are the best methods of construction being used?
- **Performance** – does the item do what it is meant to?
- **Safety** – will the item be safe to use?
- **Durability** – will the item last for a reasonable time?
- **Aesthetic properties** – does the item look good?

These areas have to be considered, no matter what the item being designed is – whether it is a food product, a textile product, or an item of equipment.

Let's look at some different products and discuss how each of the design areas listed above is important.

Product 1: Tomato soup quick snack pot

As well as the factors shown here, the consumer would also consider the factors in the chart below, and everyone will have their own preferences.

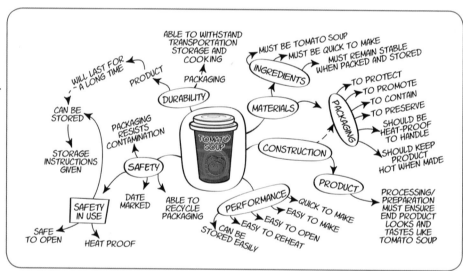

FACTOR	REASON FOR INFLUENCE
Appearance	Does the product look nice? Will I be tempted to buy it and eat it?
Colour	Does the colour look nice and encourage me to eat the product? Does the colour of the product reflect its name (e.g. tomato soup should not be green)?
Fashionable	Some foods become fashionable and are popular with different groups. Some sports drinks have become fashionable, so people buy them for this reason.
Likes and dislikes	If buying for your family, you will only buy food that you know your family like and will eat
Family and peer pressure	There may be a reluctance to buy certain types of food if it has never been tried before. You may decide to eat certain products (e.g. vegetarian food) because your friends are doing this.
Personal and family beliefs and values	There may be religious, cultural and moral reasons for not choosing certain foods.

Product 2: Textile items

When talking about materials to be used for textile items, it is important to know that different fibres have different **properties**. When fibres are used to make fabrics, the types and quantities of fibres combined together will give the end-product different properties. The table on page 74 summarises the main properties of different types of fibres.

Property: distinctive feature or quality.

When making a textile item, the designer has to think about the properties that the item will need, such as those listed in the table below.

PROPERTY	DESCRIPTION
Strength	How strong is the fabric? Is it made with a strong fibre or a weak and delicate fibre?
Durability	How hard-wearing is the fabric? Can it take a lot of rubbing, washing, ironing, for example?
Ease of laundering	How easily can the fabric be cared for? Can it be machine-washed or does it have to be dry-cleaned?
Absorbency	How much moisture can the fabric absorb?
Stain resistance	How resistant is the fabric is to staining? Some fabrics can be treated to make them stain resistant.
Crease resistance	How well does the fabric resist creasing, both when wearing and when laundering?
Flammability	How flame resistant is the fabric? Some fabrics can be specially treated.
Water repellence	The ability to prevent the absorption of water.
Elasticity	The ability of the fabric to stretch.
Breathability	The ability to let moisture out, but not let water in.
Insulation/warmth	The ability to keep warmth around the body.

Different items, such as a jacket for hill walking and a sports shirt require different properties. All of these properties will be determined by the properties of the materials that the designer used when planning the product. This may involve the use of only one type of fibre or a combination of several types of fibre.

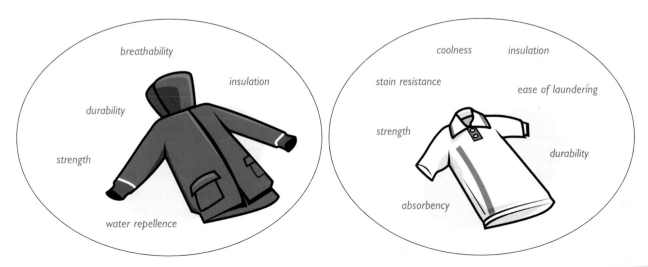

FIBRE TYPE	PROPERTY							
	ABSORBENCY	DURABILITY	STRENGTH	WARMTH	RESISTANCE TO CREASING	ELASTICITY	FLAME RESISTANCE	EASE OF WASHING
Cotton	*****	*****	****	**	*	***	*	****
Linen	*****	*****	*****	***	*	*	*	**
Silk	*****	*****	****	****	**	***	***	*
Wool	*****	*	*	*****	*****	*****	***	*
Acrylic	***	***	****	*****	*****	*****	*	****
Polyester	*	*****	*****	**	*****	***	****	****
Nylon	*	*****	*****	*	****	*****	****	****
Viscose	*****	*	***	*	*	*	*	***
Acetate	****	*	***	*	***	***	***	***
Elastane	*	*****	****	**	*****	*****	*	****

* = poor; ***** = good

Notes
- Elastane is a stretchy fibre made from a substance called **polyurethane**.
- Cotton, wool, silk and linen are all **natural** fibres.
- Polyester, nylon, rayon, viscose, acetate and elastane are classified as **synthetic** fibres or man-made fibres.

Different fibres can be combined together to improve the overall performance of a fabric. For example, polyester and cotton are often combined and used in the production of fabric for shirts and blouses. Polyester brings the fabric some of the properties, such as crease-resistance, that cotton lacks. Cotton provides properties, such as absorbency and warmth, that polyester lacks.

Special finishes and fabrics

Fabrics can have special finishes added to them in order to improve their performance. Some examples include:

- **Flameproof** finish – added to cotton and linen for furnishing fabrics
- **Waterproof** finish – added to cotton, wool, silk and linen for clothing
- **Stain-resistant** finish – can be added to most fabrics

- **Shrink-resistant** finish – can be added to cotton and wool for clothing
- **Antistatic** finish – can be added to nylon and polyester used for underwear.

Special fabrics have now been designed that incorporate specially developed fibres, which can be used to make lightweight fabrics and have a variety of uses. One example is Trevira Finesse – a polyester fabric. It is made from very fine fibres which are lightly woven together, leaving the fabric with very small pores. This prevents the fabric from becoming wet, while still allowing vapour from perspiration to pass through.

Gore-Tex® is a special **membrane** which consists of millions of tiny holes, small enough to keep rain out but large enough to let water vapour from perspiration out. This makes the membrane especially suitable for use in sportswear.

For you to do

3 **a** Which fibre(s) has the best rating for flame resistance?

  b Which fibre(s) has the worst rating for strength?

  c Which fibre(s) would you use if you needed absorbency and resistance to creasing?

  d Why would you not use viscose as a main fibre for an outdoor winter jacket?

Product 3: Child's football top

What factors would you consider when buying a football top for a child (or any other item of clothing?

New technology

As modern technology develops, manufacturers are finding new ways to make fabric and clothing much more exciting and innovative. Some examples are described here.

Lumalive textiles have flexible arrays of coloured light-emitting diodes (LEDs) fully integrated into the fabric – making it possible to create fabrics that can carry constantly changing images and messages.

Gorix is a new electroconductive fabric that adjusts to the wearer's own temperature, so it not only warms the wearer but reacts to their body heat to maintain a desired temperature without overheating.

New textiles are being developed to be worn by surgeons as they operate in hospital: the fabrics are designed to be breathable (improving the comfort of the wearer) and to prevent bacteria from moving from the surgeon to the patient.

PROPERTY	DESCRIPTION
Appearance	Does the product look good? Does it resemble a football top? Will I be tempted to buy it and wear it?
Colour	Does the colour look good and encourage me to buy the product? Are there a variety of colours available so that I can buy one that matches my favourite team? Does the item have to coordinate with other items I have (e.g. football shorts)?
Fashionable	Is the product fashionable and something that I want to wear? Many teenagers and young people are keen to wear what are considered the most fashionable 'labels', i.e. designer clothing.
Likes and dislikes	If you do not like the look or colour of the product, you will have to keep on looking around different shops.
Family and peer pressure	In some households, parents buy clothes for their children; their taste in what is acceptable or not may differ from their children's. This may be a purchase to 'be like your friends' if they have similar tops.
Personal and family beliefs and values	Certain religions and cultures have special rules about clothing. Some families may not buy clothing if it has been made in countries which they have ethical or moral concerns about, such as those with a dubious human rights record or where children are forced to work in slave labour conditions to manufacture the clothing.

CONSERVATION OF RESOURCES

The conservation of resources is an additional factor that many people take into account when considering the choice of materials and equipment. In particular, there are two main areas to be considered:

- conservation of energy and reduction of running costs
- using recycled/recyclable and second-hand goods.

Conservation of energy and reduction of running costs

Conservation of energy is all about trying to reduce the amount of energy that you use in the home. This also includes choosing electrical equipment that uses energy wisely and has low running costs. There are some simple rules that you can follow to save energy in different parts of the home.

- If your boiler is more than 15 years old it will be less efficient than a modern one. Modern boilers use less fuel to produce the same amount of heat. Replacing an old boiler could take one-fifth off your fuel bills.
- Draughts enter your home in gaps around doors, windows and floors, accounting for up to 20% of lost heat. Wherever you can feel cold air coming in, warm air is going out. Draft exclusion strips can be placed around draughty windows and doors.
- Double-glazing cuts heat loss with the help of air trapped in the gap between the two panes of glass. This air doesn't mix with the air in the room or that outside, and so creates an insulating barrier. This also reduces noise and condensation problems.
- Loft insulation that is 20 cm thick can cut 20% off heating bills.
- Walls lose more heat than any other part of your home – consider cavity wall insulation.
- Ordinary light bulbs use up to six times as much electricity as energy-saving alternatives. Energy-

saving light bulbs use electronics that enable them to produce light using a fraction of the energy.

- By insulating your hot water tank and pipes, you will retain hot water for longer, and save money on heating it. Insulate pipes if you can – especially between the boiler and the hot water cylinder if you have one.
- The technology used in new electrical appliances generally means they use less electricity, and less water and detergents (if washing appliance).

> **Did you know?**
> - The average household electricity bill is £383 per year. By reducing your thermostat by 1.25°C you can save £38.30 per year.
> - The average household wastes £37 each year by leaving appliances such as televisions, videos, stereos, computers, and cordless phones on standby.
> - Energy-efficient light bulbs last 12 times longer than standard light bulbs. For each bulb you fit, you can save up to £9 on your annual electricity bill.
> - A shower uses only two-fifths of the water needed for a bath.

Internet activity

4 Visit the website of the Energy Saving Trust, select 'What can I do today', then select 'Cheap and simple tips' or 'Top ten tips'. Make a list of the things you and your family could do to use less energy around the house.

Links to this site and other websites relating to Standard Grade Home Economics can be found at:

Simple energy-saving tips

- Always remember to turn off the lights when you leave a room.
- Always remember to put the plug in a basin or sink. Leaving hot water taps running without the plug in is wasteful.
- Choose the right size pan for the food and cooker, and keep lids on when cooking. Don't use any more water than you need.
- Don't overfill the kettle; just heat the amount of water you really need – the kettle will boil more quickly.
- When using the washing machine wait until you have a full load before using, or use the half load or economy programme if your machine has one.
- Most modern washing powders work effectively at lower temperatures, so unless you have very dirty clothes to wash, try using the low temperature programme.
- If you have a tumble-drier, avoid filling it with really wet clothes – wring them out or spin-dry them first.
- With dishwashers, try using a low-temperature programme unless there are some really dirty dishes to tackle.
- Close your curtains in the evening to stop heat escaping through the windows.
- If you are going away for a few days, leave the thermostat on a low setting to provide protection from freezing without costing too much.

Microwave ovens

- The higher the wattage, the quicker the cooking time
- Microwave ovens use less energy than conventional cookers

Cookers

- Different-sized burners or rings suit different pan sizes
- Thermostatically controlled oven – ensures correct temperature
- Fan oven ensures even cooking and can also reduce cooking times
- Full and half-width grilling facility – useful when grilling small portions
- Top oven for use when cooking smaller portions
- Programmable times for oven – can allow cooking of food when fuel is cheaper
- Heat flow/zoned heat system in the oven allows simultaneous cooking of dishes that require different temperatures

Washing machines

- Delay start programme – machine can be set to start early in the morning when fuel is cheaper
- Detergent recycling system – saves excess use of detergents
- Automatic water level control – adjusts the level of water used according to the wash load
- Half-load cycle for small wash loads – saves energy and water use
- Economy wash cycle – uses less energy and water
- Quick wash cycle – shorter wash time, using less energy and water
- Energy save (no heat) cycle – saves energy
- High spin speed leaves clothing drier, reducing tumble drying time and so saving energy

Tumble-driers

- Variable heat settings – can save energy cost
- Delay start programme – machine can be set to start early in the morning when fuel is cheaper
- Sensor dry feature – automatically stops when clothes are dry, saving energy
- Reverse tumble dry – speeds up drying process, saving energy
- Ecosensor – automatically switches to a cool cycle when clothes are dry

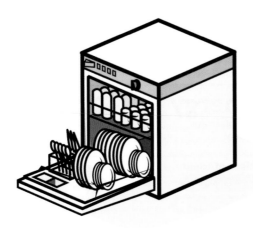

Dishwashers

- Economy wash programme – saves energy
- Rapid wash cycle – quicker washing uses less water and energy
- Cold prewash – saves energy as water is not heated
- Temperature selection – selects a lower temperature to save energy

Buying equipment

When purchasing equipment, there are a number of things we can do to ensure we are buying equipment which will conserve energy and reduce running costs. In particular there are a number of design features built into modern appliances that will help to conserve energy.

Labelling and energy rating systems

Many appliances now have **energy rating systems** that consumers can use to help them compare the energy efficiency of similar products.

The Energy Labelling Directive requires that appliances be labelled to show their power consumption in such a way that it is possible to compare the efficiency of each appliance with that of other makes and models. It is thought that consumers will prefer more energy-efficient appliances to those that use more energy. The Directive covers the following appliances:

- washing machines
- electric tumble-driers
- refrigerators and freezers
- combined washer-driers
- dishwashers
- light bulbs.

The scheme labels products according to the amount of energy they use. Products are rated on a 7-point scale, as shown.

The washing and drying performances for washing machines, dishwashers and tumble-driers are rated using this same 7-point scale.

In addition, appliance labels now give a more detailed breakdown of their performance as shown by the examples on page 80.

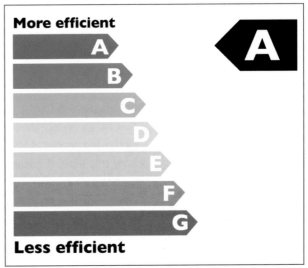

Washing machine

Energy efficiency	Class A
Energy consumption	0·95 kWh/cycle
Washing performance	A
Spin drying performance	C
Max. spin speed	1000 RPM
Capacity (cotton)	5 kg (11 lbs)
Water consumption	59 litres
Estimated annual consumption:	
Energy	190 kWh/year
Water	11800 litres

Fridge

Energy efficiency	Class C
Energy consumption	347 kWh/year

Fridge freezer

Energy efficiency	Class A
Energy consumption	365 kWh/year

Dishwasher

Energy efficiency	Class D
Energy consumption	1·6 kWH/cycle
Washing performance	B
Drying performance	C
Water consumption	19 litres

Knowing these facts and figures can be good for the consumer, as they can use this information to make valid comparisons between similar products and select the products that best suit their needs.

The Energy Saving Recommended label

The Energy Saving Trust encourages people to

use energy wisely by purchasing products that carry this label. It means the product is more energy efficient than some other models. By using less energy, it saves you money and benefits the environment.

Certification mark

For you to do

5 Study the label below an answer the questions that follow.

Energy Manufacturer Model	**Washing machine**	
More efficient		
A		**B**
B		
C		
D		
E		
F		
G		
Less efficient		
Energy consumption kWh/cycle	**1.75**	
(Based on standard test results for 60°C cotton cycle) Actual energy consumption will depend on how the appliance is used		
Washing performance A: higher G: lower	**A**BCDEFG	
Spin drying performance A: higher G: lower Spin speed (rpm)	A**B**CDEFG 1400	
Capacity (cotton) kg Water consumption	5.0 5.5	
Noise (dB(A) re 1pW)	Washing Spinning	5.2 7.6
Further information contained in product brochure		

a What appliance did this label come from?

b What energy rating does this appliance have?

c Is this a good rating? Explain.

d What is the washing performance rating for this appliance?

e What is the spin drying performance rating for this appliance?

f Why might information about noise be important for a consumer?

g If you had a water meter and you have to pay for all the water you use in your house, what item of information on this label would be important? Explain.

Recycled/recyclable goods

The use of **recycled** products/components and the option of recycling products is an important design feature.

Using recycled and second-hand products saves precious resources and reduces the need to use **landfill sites**. Recycling is the process of recovering and reusing waste products. Many people are concerned about making good use of the resources that we have available and, where possible, trying not to waste these. We can recycle many household products ranging from computer ink cartridges and paper to textiles and glass bottles, and so reduce the burden on the environment. Products that are recycled in large quantities include paper, cardboard, metals, glass, plastic and food waste.

WORD BANK

Landfill site: a place where local authorities and industry can take waste so that it can be buried.

Recycling household items and materials

Many local councils now offer a recycling service and supply households with special recycling bins that can be used to separate different types of household waste. Once collected, the **refuse** (rubbish) is then sorted before being sent on for recycling. The chart below shows the main methods of recycling common household waste.

MATERIAL	WAYS TO RECYCLE
Glass	Glass items can be taken to a bottle bank so they can be recycled.
	Bottles and jars can be reused for storing other foods or items.
Paper	Paper can be taken to a paper bank where it can be recycled or uplifted by the local council.
Steel can (most food cans)	These can be taken to special steel can banks for recycling.
Aluminium (most drink cans)	These can be taken to aluminium banks where they can be recycled to make new cans.
	Many schools and offices have special recycling boxes for aluminium cans.
Plastic	Some plastics can be recycled, but the different types of plastic need to be separated.
	Symbols can now be found on plastic packaging materials to allow for the separation of different types of plastic.
	There tend to be fewer collection facilities for plastic materials.
	Plastic carrier bags can be reused.
	Plastic pots and bottles can be used to make craft items.
Food waste	Food waste can be used in a compost heap.
Textiles	Textiles can be taken to a textile recycling centre where they can be used in a variety of ways including making new fabrics.
	They can be taken to a charity shop where they can be reused/resold.
	Clothing and blankets can be taken to charity shops which redistribute them both home and abroad.
	Old clothes can be redesigned into new clothes or cut up and used for patchwork and appliqué.
	Buttons, zips and trimmings can be removed and reused.

Recycling labels

The packaging on most products displays labels or symbols which provide useful information about recycling. The most commonly used recycling labels are shown below.

Consumers can also look at the labels of products they are considering buying. Most products will indicate:

- if they have used recycled materials during production
- if they can be recycled once used.

Moebius loop	**Moebius loop with percentage**	**Recyclable aluminium**
This packaging is capable of being recycled.	This packaging contains x% of recycled material.	This product is made from aluminium which can be recycled.
Recyclable steel	**Recyclable glass**	**Recyclable plastic**
This product is made from steel which can be recycled.	The product or packaging can be disposed of in a glass bottle bank.	PETE HDPE V LDPE PP PS OTHER
National Association of Paper Merchants	**Tidyman**	Different types of plastic need to be separated before they can be recycled – the number will range from 1 (for polyethylene terepthalate (PETE) type plastics) to 7 (for all other resins and multi-materials).
The product/packaging is made from a minimum of 75% genuine paper waste and/or board fibre.	Used to encourage people to dispose of litter carefully and thoughtfully.	

For you to do

6 Study the pie chart and answer the following questions.

a What percentage of household waste comes from:
- garden waste
- textiles
- plastics

b What is the most common type of waste in the average UK household?

c Nappies account for 2% of household waste. Forty years ago, nappies would have accounted for 0%. Explain the increase.

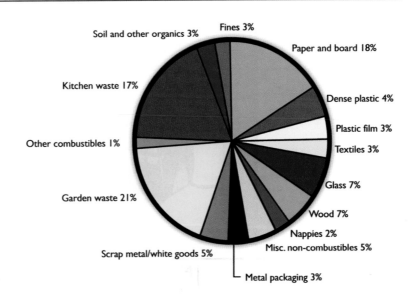

Soil and other organics 3%
Fines 3%
Paper and board 18%
Kitchen waste 17%
Dense plastic 4%
Plastic film 3%
Other combustibles 1%
Textiles 3%
Glass 7%
Garden waste 21%
Wood 7%
Nappies 2%
Misc. non-combustibles 5%
Scrap metal/white goods 5%
Metal packaging 3%

Buying second-hand goods

A recent survey by a large insurance company showed that one in seven items in the average UK home is second hand. More than 9.5 million home-owners now go to car boot sales and charity shops looking for a bargain. The existence of the second-hand market means that consumers can dispose of items they no longer need but the items are made available for use by someone else. This helps to reduce landfill sites. However, you need to be careful when buying second-hand goods as a considerable number of electrical goods sold second hand can be faulty and therefore potentially dangerous, according to another report by an insurance company.

Quick Quiz

I Look at the backpack. Choose which design feature or features would be best for each of the following situations.

	SITUATION		FEATURE
a	Person wishing to carry heavy weight	**I**	Bright fluorescent colours
b	Person sailing	**2**	Adjustable shoulder straps
c	Person carrying house keys and money	**3**	Secure zipped inner-pocket
d	Person walking at night	**4**	Padded shoulder straps
e	Backpack for a youth club where different people will be using it	**5**	Adjustable straps which strap around your waist
		6	Waterproof fabric
		7	Lightweight fabric

2 Match each energy-saving feature to the correct appliance.

	APPLIANCE		ENERGY SAVING FEATURE
1	Washing machine	**a**	Fan assisted
2	Tumble drier	**b**	High wattage
3	Dishwasher	**c**	High spin speed
4	Microwave cooker	**d**	Reverse tumble
5	Oven	**e**	Cold prewash

CHAPTER 7: PHYSICAL NEEDS OF INDIVIDUALS AND FAMILIES

In this chapter

- Clothing
- Shelter
- Reliable sources of consumer advice
- Consumer rights and responsibilities
- Labelling of products
- General wellbeing

CLOTHING

We are all individuals who have different needs and wants. Just as we all look different, we all have different physical needs. Earlier sections of this book have looked at the food needs of individuals and families. This section considers our different needs for clothing.

Why do we need clothing? One reason is **protection**.

Protection

- Protect us from the elements – rain, sun, snow and wind

- Protect us from being embarrassed so that we are not naked

- Some clothing can protect us from other dangers (e.g. fire)

Other reasons for wearing clothing include:

- safety – firemen wear protective clothing
- occupation – some (e.g. police) require a uniform
- status – clothing can be used to show the wearer's position in society or an organisation
- comfort – some clothes are worn for comfort.

Velcro: material that consists of two strips of nylon fabric that stick together, used to fasten clothes.

The needs of different groups

Different groups and individuals have particular needs for clothing and footwear.

Babies

Babies find it difficult to control and maintain their body temperatures. For this reason they should be dressed in several layers of thin clothing which can easily be added to or removed in order to help maintain body temperature. For example, in warmer weather the number of layers should be reduced to prevent overheating.

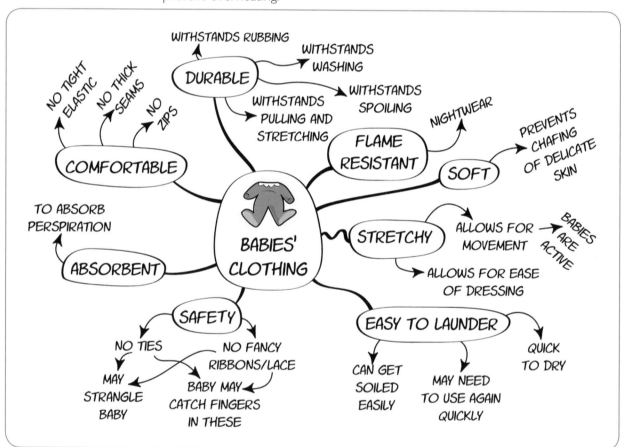

Design features to consider:

- Are fastenings easy to use (e.g. poppers and **Velcro**)?
- Baby-grows are good as they meet most of the requirements shown in the mind-map above.
- Trousers can be padded at the knees to prevent **chafing** (rubbing) when crawling.
- Babies do not need shoes until they start walking. Shoes must fit well so that they support the baby's feet and do not cause the feet to become **deformed** or mis-shapen. Ideally have the baby's feet measured regularly.
- Baby-grows and socks must fit well.

Toddlers and young children

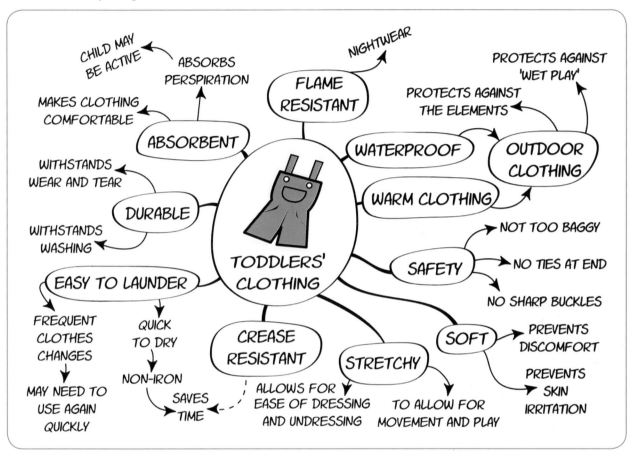

Design features to consider:

- May still be wearing nappies, so access for changing is important – dungarees or trousers with leg poppers.
- Elasticated waistbands – allow for ease of dressing/undressing.
- Fastenings – easy to use (e.g. Velcro and large buttons encourage independence when dressing).
- Clothing should allow for stretching and movement when playing (e.g. jogger bottoms).
- Jackets should not have neck ties, etc. which may cause an accident.
- Nightwear should allow freedom of movement and comfort.
- Footwear and socks should fit well. A shoe shop can provide specialist advice.
- Velcro fastenings on footwear encourage independence.

Adolescents and teenagers

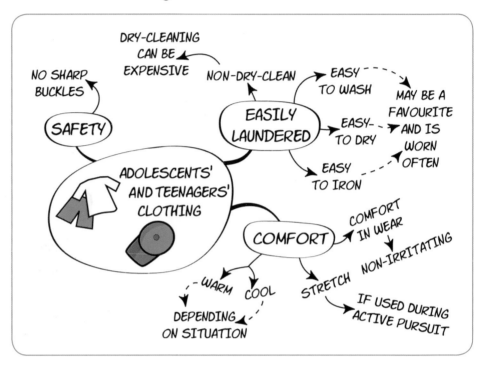

Design features to consider:
- The above mind-map for teenagers' and adolescents' clothing is much smaller than those of other groups. This is because what teenagers will buy will be dependent on many different factors that we have already discussed. These include cost, colour, peer pressure and family pressure.
- Teenagers are often involved in a variety of differing activities so clothing may need to be **multifunctional**.
- One of the trends of the past 20 years has been an increase in the purchase of designer clothing by teenagers.
- There is now a move from some teenagers to move away from designer clothing to non-branded clothes and accessories.
- Some clothing defy normal conventions (e.g. oversized or baggy clothing or extreme high heels).
- Fashions tend to be cyclical. Most fashions come and go, so clothing bought to meet a fashion trend may not remain fashionable.
- Footwear should fit well – even allowing for fashion!

Adults

Clothing for adults will vary from individual to individual. There are no particular design features that are particular to adults. The properties required from clothing will be determined by the factors that we have already discussed such as income, size, and lifestyle (including employment requirements).

Elderly people

The elderly person may not have any particular requirements for clothing.
Many elderly people lead very active and full lives. Others may have problems
with mobility; some may have particular illnesses, such as arthritis, and these
will pose particular requirements for elderly people when considering clothing.

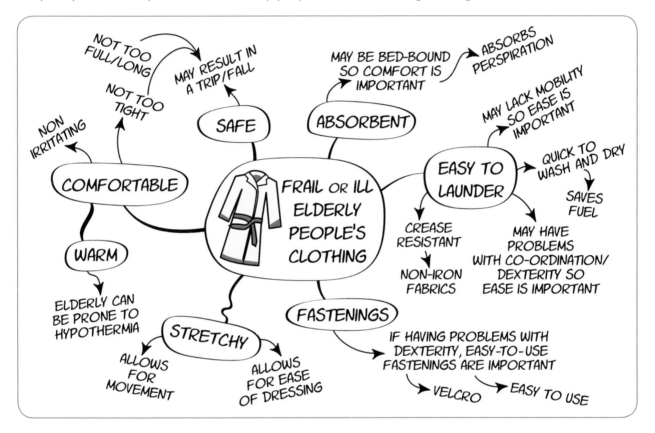

Design features to consider:

- These will vary from individual to individual.
- Elasticated waistbands may help make dressing easier if mobility or dexterity
  is a problem.
- Front-fastening garments may be easier to use than back-fastening garments.
- Outdoor clothing should be warm and prevent draughts (e.g. elasticated
  cuffs and waistband).
- People who lack mobility may have problems keeping warm. They should be
  encouraged to wear several thin layers of clothing, wear thermal underwear
  and if necessary a hat and gloves.
- Shoes should fit properly – flat shoes are ideal.
- Shoes should be maintained to ensure they have good grips to prevent
  slipping.
- Slip-on shoes are easy to put on with little physical effort needed from
  bending down or tying laces, so are helpful to individuals who suffer from
  arthritis or other conditions.

Pregnant and breastfeeding women

During pregnancy, women become larger and heavier. Mobility may also be reduced in the later stages of pregnancy. There are a number of factors that need to be considered when selecting clothing for pregnant women:

- Clothing should be loose fitting to allow for comfort, movement and growth.
- Elasticated bands improve comfort and support.
- Fastenings should be able to be adjusted to provide comfort.
- Fabric should be soft and stretchy to accommodate the increased body size and provide comfort.
- Clothing should be easy to launder as this will prevent having to purchase many clothes.
- Shoes should provide support and fit well as there is extra weight to be carried.
- Flat shoes are ideal.
- When breastfeeding, garments which allow easy access for breastfeeding are important.

Individuals with physical disabilities

The individual needs of those with physical disabilities will vary depending on the type of disability. The needs of a person with a broken arm vary considerably from those of a person with limited sight.

Properties of textiles

When thinking about the properties of textiles for clothing and footwear, there are a number of different factors that need to be considered:

- protection
- comfort and fit
- suitability for purpose
- safety.

Protection

We use textiles to protect us from the environment. Textiles keep us cool, warm and dry. When we wear clothing we tend to adjust what we wear to suit different climatic conditions and so suit the environment in which we will be wearing the clothes, that is, indoor or outdoor.

Keeping warm, keeping cool, keeping dry

In order to keep the body warm, clothing must be able to insulate the body. This can be achieved by trapping a layer of air inside the clothing.

When we wear clothes and take part in activities, we perspire. Clothing has an important role to play in the removal of this perspiration. Some fabrics can absorb this moisture and then release the moisture to the outside where it evaporates.

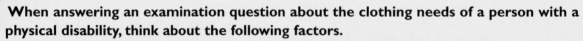

When answering an examination question about the clothing needs of a person with a physical disability, think about the following factors.

- **What is the physical disability?**
- **How will this affect the clothing to be purchased?**
- **Are there problems with dressing? (If so, stretch and fastening are important.)**
- **Is the person mobile? (You need to think about safety, absorbency and ease of laundering.)**
- **Will the garment be subject to particular stresses, for example, rubbing? (If so, durability is an important consideration.)**

You will need to think about the problem carefully and plan your answer before writing. Remember that the question paper contains space for rough work. Use this space to plan your answer.

There are a number of ways of using the properties of textiles to help keep us warm, cool or dry.

- **Layering** – when faced with cold climatic conditions, wearing a number of thin layers of clothing can help maintain warmth. Each layer of clothing will trap air and so insulate the body.
- **Fibres** – some fibres can trap air and so are naturally warm (e.g. wool). Other fibres naturally absorb moisture and so help to keep the body dry (e.g. cotton).
- **Fabric construction** – this can affect the amount of air trapped. Knitted products, for example, trap larger amounts of air and so tend to insulate the body well.
- **Fabric finishing** – some fabrics can be treated to help them retain warmth or repel water.

Special fibres and finishes
Quilting
This is often used on duvets and anoraks, as it offers good insulation. Wadding is sewn between two layers of fabric, and traps a large amount of air, providing a good insulating layer.

Fleece fabrics
These are used in sweatshirts, dressing gowns and outdoor jackets. These are lightweight fabrics, which have a fleecy soft backing which is comfortable to the skin. Air is trapped in this fleece backing and so keeps the body warm.

Microfibres
These are very fine synthetic fibres. They can be used alone or mixed with other fibres. These microfibres are ideal for waterproof products. The fibres are woven tightly creating small air traps, which prevent rain and wind getting in but at the same time allow water vapour from the body to escape. This results in both warmth and dryness in clothing which makes the fabric suitable for all types of outdoor clothing (e.g. hillwalking jackets, ski wear).

Microporous membranes
These are membranes (very thin pieces of fabric) with tiny holes, which can be applied to a wide range of fabrics. These membranes prevent water and wind getting into the clothing, but allow perspiration to travel to the outside of the clothing where it can evaporate. This helps to keep the body dry and warm.

Design features
There are specific design features that can be added to garments to assist in keeping you warm, cool or dry.

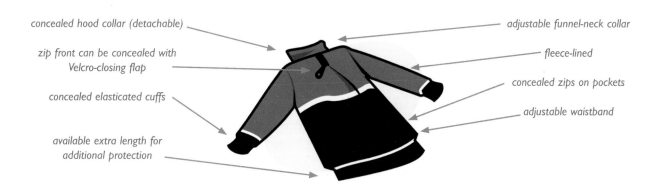

concealed hood collar (detachable)

zip front can be concealed with Velcro-closing flap

concealed elasticated cuffs

available extra length for additional protection

adjustable funnel-neck collar

fleece-lined

concealed zips on pockets

adjustable waistband

Comfort and fit

As well as thinking about protection, we need to consider comfort and fit when selecting clothes. There are a number of factors that affect comfort.

For more information about the specific properties of textiles and fibres, see page 74.

FACTOR	EXPLANATION
Softness	How the fabric feels to the touch. Some fabrics, such as silk and fleece, feel very soft and smooth when next to the skin, while others might tickle or scratch.
Absorbency	Fibres that can absorb moisture (perspiration) from the skin, and then carry this moisture to the outside of the clothing to evaporate, will aid comfort. Some synthetic fibres have poor absorbency and can lead to a feeling of **clamminess** or wetness.
Weight	The weight of the fabric can assist with comfort. Some of the newer fleece sports tops are designed to be very lightweight while still keeping you warm and dry. This is important for activities such as hillwalking where added weight could lead to discomfort.
Elasticity	Elasticity is an important property for some garments. For activities and sports where the body needs to be able to move and stretch easily, it is important that clothes do not restrict freedom of movement. Such clothing allows stretching, and also retains its shape. Garments which have **elastane** added to them also tend to hug the body. This is useful in a swimming costume which needs to be drag-resistant so helping to improve performance.
Size	When a garment is too tight in certain areas (e.g. the waist), it can lead to a feeling of discomfort. We are not all the same size and so clothes tend to come in a variety of sizes. Specialist shops are available for people who are outside the normal range of sizes. Some garments, such as jeans, are now produced using fibres including a small amount of **elastomeric** fibres. This provides a degree of stretch which can aid comfort.
Fastenings	There are many different types of fastening available. Manufacturers are usually careful in selecting fastenings which are appropriate to the garment and which aid comfort. Fastenings or labels which are inappropriately placed can lead to discomfort and irritation of the skin. It is always advisable to try clothing on before buying to ensure a good fit, but also to determine comfort. Fastenings should be easy to use. The type of fastening used is determined by the item. Zips, for example, would not be appropriate for a baby-grow as they are less flexible than poppers.
Crease resistance	We can feel uncomfortable if we feel that we are inappropriately dressed. Having clothing that is crease-free can be important in terms of feeling comfortable in the clothing that you are wearing. If you are packing clothing for a holiday, crease-resistant clothing will prevent you from having to pack a travel iron. Likewise, crease-resistant clothing is suitable if you are involved in an occupation where you are sitting for a long period of time.

Footwear considerations

Footwear should fit well. If it is to be comfortable, it is always advisable to get your feet measured before you buy new shoes. Many shoes come in different sizes and width fittings to ensure your comfort. Think about the following:

- Shoes which are made of natural materials allow feet to breathe.
- The grip on the shoes should be good to prevent slipping. This becomes more important if the shoes are to be used for many sports or specific activities such as hillwalking.
- Shoes should support and protect your feet. Your feet carry the weight of your whole body.
- Some footwear have adjustable fastenings, which can aid comfort.
- Outdoor shoes should be waterproof.
- Some trainers are made from breathable fabrics, which allow the feet to breathe and stay fresh and comfortable.
- Some trainers now incorporate visible air sole units, which protect the feet when playing sports.

For you to do

1 A young male is training for a marathon race. He is planning to go running in the evenings. What specific design features do you think he might have to consider when buying a running jacket? (If you need some help, type 'running jackets' into a web search engine.)
2 By either visiting a shop or using the internet or mail-order catalogues, make a list of all the new design features that can be found in training shoes.

Suitability for purpose

Sometimes we select clothes for a particular occasion:

- for work
- for leisure
- for special occasions (e.g. a wedding).

When choosing clothing, it is important to think about the following factors:

- What will the item be used for?
- Will it require any special properties (e.g. flame/ crease-resistance)?
- Are there any special design features it will need (e.g. pockets to carry objects)?
- Are there any other factors that you need to think about (e.g. colour, cost)?

Safety

Safety is always an important consideration when buying textile items. There are a number of safety factors that you should think about.

Fabrics can be treated to make them **flameproof**. The fabric is treated with a chemical which will prevent the item catching fire if it is placed near a naked flame. Many fabrics used for soft furnishings (such as sofa beds and cushions) and nightwear are treated to stop them burning. The British Standards Institution lays down strict guidelines on the way fabrics should be produced for both nightwear and soft furnishings. These items will display a **low flammability** label or other appropriate warnings. Here are two examples:

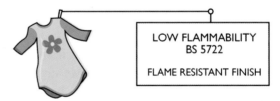

label found on a child's nightdress

label found on a boy's pyjamas

Dressing gowns and nightdresses tend to be loose fitting and so are at risk of catching fire from a naked flame (e.g. a living room fire).

Many people get confused between flammability and inflammability.

- ***Flammable*** describes something that burns easily
- ***Inflammable*** describes something that burns very easily
- ***Non-flammable*** describes something that cannot burn or is very difficult to burn

RESISTANT
Complies with BS: 7177:1996 for domestic use (low hazard)

This is an example of a label found attached to a sofa bed. These safety labels must be permanently attached to the product in addition to removable swing labels.

This product has been tested and meets the tests undertaken for flammability resistance.

This symbol means that the covers and fillings are cigarette- and match-resistant.

There are other factors that affect the safety of textile items.

- Fabrics which trap air, such as knits or brushed surfaces, tend to be more flammable.
- Wools and silks are generally flame-resistant, whereas cotton, linen and viscose are all flammable.
- Luminous or reflective strips can be added to clothing and accessories to ensure visibility, especially in dim light.
- Bright colours are often used on hillwalking and mountaineering clothing to ensure visibility.
- Some fabrics can be coated (e.g. PVC-coated aprons are often used in kitchens to protect against splashes).

SHELTER

It is important that individuals and families have shelter, in whatever form this takes. We require shelter to protect us from the weather and to provide safe and secure places to live. Most forms of shelter provide us with the basic essentials that we need to ensure survival:

- warmth – generated from gas, electricity or oil
- water – provided directly to most forms of shelter
- provision of toilet facilities.

There are very many different types of shelter available to an individual. The type of shelter used will be determined by many different factors.

TYPE OF SHELTER	DESCRIPTION
Student accommodation	Can be a shared flat, a room within a private home or a room provided in halls of residence – usually self-catering.
Accommodation linked to job	Some jobs come with accommodation provided. If you are in the army, for example, housing can be provided either in a dormitory if you are single, or in an army house if you have a partner or family. When you leave the job, you also have to leave your accommodation.
Temporary accommodation	For some people, finding accommodation can be difficult. Temporary or short-term accommodation is provided both by local authorities and charities.
Flats and houses	For many people a flat or house is the main form of accommodation. They can be provided by the local authority, by housing associations or can be privately rented or owned.
Caravans and mobile homes	For some people, caravans and mobile homes are suitable forms of accommodation – either temporarily or permanently.
Sheltered housing	Housing can become a major issue for the elderly if they are finding it difficult to remain independent. Sheltered accommodation is specially designed for elderly people or people with disabilities. This form of accommodation has a form of supervision where a warden is available if help or assistance is required.
Other forms	<ul><li>For reasons of ill health, nursing homes and hospitals may be a form of shelter – either temporarily or permanently.</li><li>Hotels and guesthouses are used to provide temporary accommodation for those who are travelling.</li></ul>

RELIABLE SOURCES OF CONSUMER ADVICE

When shopping for goods and services, there are times when you think it would be good to know a little more about your rights and responsibilities as a consumer. There are times when you might think that it would be good to have someone to talk to who can provide you with help and advice on consumer matters. There is a lot of help and interesting information available on consumer issues.

The bodies and organisations described on pages 96–98 offer consumer advice. This advice is generally very reliable and up to date. These agencies all offer different types of advice and support.

Citizens Advice Bureau

The Citizens Advice Bureau (CAB) service offers free, independent and confidential advice. The CAB helps solve problems which are central to people's lives, including debt and consumer issues, benefits, housing, legal matters, employment, and immigration. Advisers can help fill out forms, write letters, negotiate with creditors and represent clients at court or tribunal. Ninety per cent of the advisers are volunteers. They include CAB advisers, administrators and management committee members.

Each CAB belongs to the National Association of Citizen's Advice Bureaux (NACAB), which sets standards for advice, training, equal opportunities and accessibility. The NACAB also produces a variety of free publications.

As well as giving advice, the NACAB uses its bank of client evidence to find out where local and national services and policies should change.

Each CAB is an independent charity, relying on funding from the local authority and from local businesses, charitable trusts and individual donations.

CABs are found in most main towns and cities. Most CABs now provide an online service. Many CABs operate on an appointment basis.

Consumers' Association

The Consumers' Association (CA) was established in 1957 to provide pre-shopping help and assistance to consumers.

The CA carries out research and undertakes comprehensive testing of consumer products, ranging from cars to washing machines. These tests are independent and the results are published in a magazine called *Which*? The CA will independently test a range of similar products (e.g. dishwashers), and report the findings to the consumer. The report will provide a wide range of information including prices, design features, test results for each product, what they regard as the best buy.

Which? magazine also provides a wide range of consumer information, ranging from issues such as the genetic modification of food to the services provided by dentists.

The CA is a strong campaigner for the rights of the consumer. It undertakes research and acts as a **pressure group** to benefit the consumer.

The CA does not handle individual complaints unless you subscribe. To obtain *Which*? magazine you have to pay a monthly subscription. You can also subscribe to an online service called 'Online Which?'. Local libraries usually have copies of *Which*? magazine.

Consumer Advice Centre

Consumer Advice Centres (CACs) can be organised by the local authority or be independent. They offer free and independent confidential advice to the consumer. Like CABs, CACs offer practical help on how you can deal with a wide range of consumer problems and issues as well as introducing you to other sources of help (e.g. organisations who can advise and assist you with specific problems). CACs can assist you with taking action and provide advice on using the Small Claims Court.

The staff at CACs are given specific training on issues relating to consumerism.

There are a number of independent CACs available and they rely on their funding from local authorities, local businesses and grants.

Many manufacturers also have consumer advice centres. These offer specific advice to consumers about the products manufactured by that company. These consumer advice centres/services are run by the manufacturers themselves; since the information isn't independent it might not be reliable.

Internet activity

3 Visit the CAB website, click on the 'Get advice' section of the website and then print out the factsheet called 'Factsheet about CAB advice'. What were the top five CAB client problems in England and Wales in 2005/06?

Links to this site and other websites relating to Standard Grade Home Economics can be found at:

For you to do

4 The next time you buy a food product or electrical product, check to see what type of customer advice/service/careline the product offers.

5 Using either a *Which?* magazine or by visiting the Which? website, answer the following questions.

a List the date of the *Which?* magazine or the date of the web-based report.

b List two different types of features reports in that issue.

c List one campaign that this issue features.

Counterfeit: fake; made to look like the original of something, usually for illegal purposes.
Pressure group: a group of people who work together to try to change the opinions and policies of the government.

Consumer Protection Department, Trading Standards Department and Environmental Health Department

Local authorities run these departments. The names given to these departments vary within each local authority. Originally these departments were split but in many areas their functions have been combined.

Consumer Protection Department and Trading Standards Department

Trading Standards Officers enforce a range of laws intended to promote fair trading, consumer protection and environmental safety.

The Trading Standards service aims to ensure that:

- members of the public are not misled by false statements about goods (including food) or about services
- consumer goods, particularly electrical appliances, toys and furniture, are constructed to high safety **specifications**
- honest traders are not put at a disadvantage by having to compete with misdescribed, **counterfeit** or dangerously shoddy goods

- the storage and sale of dangerous products such as petroleum, explosives and poisons do not put the public or environment at risk
- overloaded lorries do not cause danger to the public or damage to roads and bridges
- certain animal diseases such as foot and mouth, bovine spongiform encephalopathy (BSE), and in particular rabies, do not enter or spread through the country.

The department provides a free and confidential advice and assistance service to anyone needing help to resolve **disputes** (or disagreements) with traders, suppliers or other commercial organisations on trading standards related matters. They can also provide advice with debt problems.

Environmental Health Department

The Environmental Health Department (EHD) is responsible for protecting and improving the environment by providing environmental public health services.

Environmental Health Officers (EHOs) carry out **statutory** enforcement and advisory work. The services provided in this area concern:

- food safety
- occupational health and safety
- public health
- pollution
- dog control
- animal health

EHOs work through inspection and enforcement — checking food standards and hygiene to prevent food poisoning, ensuring housing standards, monitoring pollution, enforcing Occupational Health and Safety regulations and running the Dog Warden and Pest Control Services.

EHOs are also involved in education rather than just enforcing the rules and they work closely with schools, community organisations and other bodies on local environment and public health issues.

National Consumer Council

The National Consumer Council (NCC) is a non-departmental public body, set up by the UK government in 1975. A large part of the NCC's funding is **grant-in-aid** from the Department of Trade and Industry. It aims to:

- promote action for furthering and safeguarding the interests of consumers
- ensure that those who take decisions which will affect consumers have balanced and authoritative views of the interests of consumers before them
- insist that the interests of all consumers, including the inarticulate and disadvantaged, are taken into account.

The NCC does not deal with individual complaints but does look at issues that concern consumers. The NCC acts as a pressure group. The NCC has a separate Scottish office.

Links to websites providing online advice and support for consumers can be found at: **www.leckieandleckie.co.uk** by clicking on the Learning Lab button and navigating to the Standard Grade Home Economics Course Notes page.

WORD BANK

Statutory: decided or controlled by law.
Grant-in-aid funding: funding direct from the government.

The following organisations and agencies will not appear in examination questions, but they are important consumer organisations designed to protect the public.

The Food Standards Agency

The Food Standards Agency (FSA) is an independent government department set up by an Act of Parliament in 2000 to protect the public's health and consumer interests in relation to food. The FSA is a UK-wide organisation but has country offices in Scotland, Northern Ireland and Wales.

In Scotland the FSA has specific responsibility for:

- food standards, nutrition and diet
- general food hygiene, fish, shellfish and milk hygiene
- hygiene controls on meat and meat products
- the regulation of animal feed
- the regulation of other food processing and production matters.

The FSA produces a lot of free advice and information for the consumer and the food industry relating to all matters of food safety and production.

Consumer Direct

The UK government has funded the development of Consumer Direct, a website which aims to provide clear, practical consumer advice on items ranging from cars to faulty household appliances.

The Food Standards Agency is sometimes referred to as the FSA. However, there is another organisation that is also known as the FSA – the Financial Services Authority. Don't get the two confused!

Internet activity

6 Visit the website of Consumer Direct. Click on the 'After you buy' icon at the top of the screen, then click on the 'Know your rights' icon at the left-hand side of the screen.

What advice does this website give if you have a faulty mobile phone which the shop is unable to replace or repair?

Links to this site and other websites relating to Standard Grade Home Economics can be found at:

LECKIE&LECKIE
Learning Lab

CONSUMER RIGHTS AND RESPONSIBILITIES

Consumer Protection Act 1987

This Act ensures consumers have rights to compensation for death or injury caused by using defective consumer goods. This Act applies not only to the person or organisation from whom the goods were purchased but also includes the manufacturer or importer. The Act establishes a 'general safety requirement', namely that all goods for domestic use must be reasonably safe, bearing in mind all the circumstances.

Powers under the Act allow suspect goods to be 'suspended' from sale for up to six months, while checks on safety are conducted. If faulty, the goods may be destroyed.

These safety provisions have been extended to cover all consumer goods and require all domestic consumer goods to be safe.

The Act regulates price indications for goods, services, accommodation or facilities. Businesses must not give consumers misleading price indications.

Sale and Supply of Goods Act 1994

This law provides the consumer with three areas of protection when buying goods and services. The goods must be:

- of satisfactory quality
- fit for the intended purpose
- as described.

When you buy goods from a shop, market stall, garage, etc., the law says they have to be of **satisfactory quality**. The satisfactory quality test includes the appearance and finish of the goods, their safety and durability. Goods must be free from **defects**, even minor ones, unless the seller has pointed them out to you, and fit for all their intended purposes – including any purpose the seller told you about.

The law also gives you a reasonable time to reject goods if they're faulty. What is 'reasonable' is not a fixed period of time but will depend on their cost and complexity. Normally you can take your purchase home and make sure it is satisfactory but, if you delay examining it or telling the seller about a fault, you may lose your right to reject it and a refund of your money.

If you let the seller try to fix the faulty goods but they don't succeed, this does not affect your legal right to reject them. If you take the goods back promptly and the seller's attempt to repair them fails, you can still reject the goods – but you must act promptly.

If you buy used goods or at a sale, your rights when are exactly the same as if you bought them new. Naturally, the law takes the view that you can't expect them to be as durable or have the same appearance and finish as new goods, but they should still work properly in relation to their age and previous usage.

The Sale and Supply of Goods to Consumers Regulations 2002

These are new European Union based regulations that update the Sale and Supply of Goods Act 1994. The aim of the regulations is to provide a minimum set of common consumer rights when faulty goods have been bought. The regulations do not apply to the purchase of services. The new regulations apply to:

- sale of goods
- supply of goods
- hire of goods
- hire purchase.

The new regulations say that a consumer is entitled to goods of satisfactory quality, taking into account any description and the price. It does not apply in cases of wear and tear, misuse, accidental damage or if a consumer decides they no longer want the item.

If the item bought proves to be faulty the consumer is entitled to:

- a full refund – if the fault is reported within a reasonable time
- a partial refund – if the consumer has enjoyed some benefit from the goods before the problem started
- a reasonable amount of compensation or damages (in Scotland this means for up to 5 years after discovery of the complaint)
- a repair
- a replacement.

Trade Descriptions Act 1968 and 1972

It is an offence to apply a **false trade description** to goods or to supply goods to which a false trade description is applied. It is an offence if an employer or trader or employee falsely describes the goods he or she is selling, for example, selling a product as organic when in fact it is not. The Act also makes it illegal for traders to knowingly mislead you about the services that they provide (e.g. advertising free delivery but then actually charging for delivery).

The Food Hygiene (Scotland) Regulations 2006

The Food Hygiene (Scotland) Regulations are new regulations introduced to ensure that food hygiene legislation in Scotland meets European Union requirements. The regulations try to ensure a minimum level of food hygiene standards across all European member states.

The Food Hygiene (Scotland) Regulations 2006 replace the following regulations:

- Food Safety (General Food Hygiene) Regulations 1995
- Food Hygiene (General) Regulations 1995
- Food Safety (Temperature Control) Regulations 1995.

These regulations are designed to ensure that all food businesses operate in a safe and hygienic manner. The regulations state that food businesses have to assess all the potential risks involved in making their products. They must do this by carrying out a **risk assessment**. A risk assessment will identify if it is possible for the food product to become contaminated. If any risks are identified, the business has to take appropriate action to prevent contamination.

The regulations state that chilled foods must be kept in a refrigerator or cool, ventilated place in order to prevent development of micro-organisms. It also states that food which is being kept hot for sale should be kept above 63°C at all times. Food which is being reheated should be raised to a temperature of at least 82°C.

The regulations also ensure that the equipment and premises that are involved in the production of food are kept very clean. They lay down specific standards that must be followed in the design and equipping of a food business in the areas of:

- premises
- equipment
- food handlers
- washing facilities
- services
- practices
- transport.

The regulations state that a food worker who is suffering from any illness that might contaminate food, such as an infected wound, skin infections, diarrhoea, etc. must report this to a supervisor.

Food Safety Act 1990

The Food Safety Act protects consumers in that it states that food must not:

- injure the health of consumers
- be unfit for human consumption – that is, it ensures that all food produced and sold is safe to eat
- be contaminated in any form.

The Act ensures that the employer and the employee:

- do not do anything to the food to make it harmful
- do not sell food that is not as is stated (e.g. selling 'steak mince' that is actually beef mince)
- do not describe food in a way that will mislead consumers.

The Act covers all food premises from shops to restaurants and applies to anyone working in a food business, whether it be a small sandwich-making stall or a large food manufacturing company. The Food Safety Act increases the powers available to enforcement agencies and increases legal powers.

For you to do

7 Which organisation would you contact in each of the following situations?

a You buy a sandwich in a shop which has mould on the crust. Which Act protects you on this occasion?

b You buy a short-sleeved shirt but when you open the packaging it is a long-sleeved shirt. Which Act protects you on this occasion?

c You see a dog fouling in a pavement outside your house.

d You want to know what would be the best mobile phone to buy for use abroad.

e You need advice about debt.

f You buy a new MP3 player but it is faulty when you get it home. Which Act protects you on this occasion?

g You are looking for some general food safety advice.

LABELLING OF PRODUCTS

This section deals with the labelling of consumer products. It details what the law requires and what is additional.

Food products

By law, a food product must show the following information:

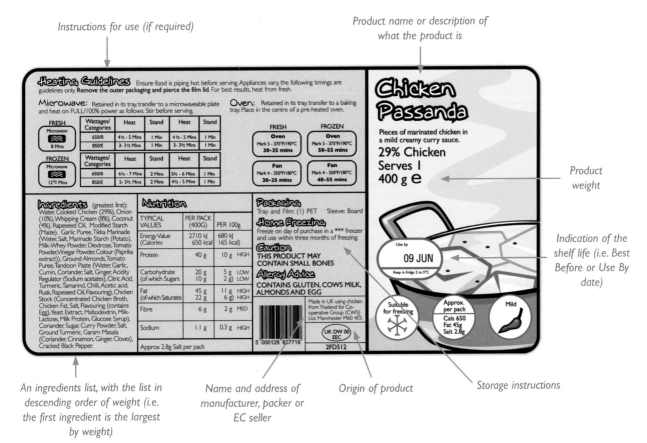

Instructions for use (if required)

Product name or description of what the product is

Product weight

Indication of the shelf life (i.e. Best Before or Use By date)

Storage instructions

Origin of product

Name and address of manufacturer, packer or EC seller

An ingredients list, with the list in descending order of weight (i.e. the first ingredient is the largest by weight)

Additional information on food labelling

- The 'e' beside the weight means that the average quantity must be accurate but the weight of each pack may vary slightly.
- In the ingredients list, any **additives** that have been used in the product must be listed, stating what their job is (e.g. potassium sorbate = preservative).
- Flavourings do not have numbers so they must be stated.
- Nutritional information is optional but most companies provide it. If it is provided, it must meet certain criteria.

- If a product makes a specific claim (e.g. 'extra fruit') the label must show the minimum amount of fruit in the product.

A manufacturer may also provide additional information for the consumer. In this example the additional information includes:

- spiciness rating (the chilli symbol)
- serving or portion size
- allergy advice
- packaging information.

Other symbols found on food products

Bar code

Bar codes are now used on most products. They are used to check the level of stock in a supermarket. When a product is sold, the bar code is scanned. This tells the supermarket that this product has been sold and allows the store to order new stock.

ISBN 1-84372-034-5

9 781843 720348

Labels to help you buy ethically

Today many people are concerned about big problems such as global warming, the extinction of species, animal testing, factory farming, exploitation of workers in less well developed countries. Some people feel that they can try to do something to reduce these problems by making good choices in the goods and services that they buy, for example, only buying free range eggs or organic vegetables.

The following symbols and information are found on food products – look out for them if you want to make ethical purchases.

Fairtrade ![Guarantees a better deal for Third World Producers FAIRTRADE] Choose products with the FAIRTRADE Mark	The Fairtrade Foundation was established in 1992 by a range of organisations and charities. Fairtrade is designed to ensure that disadvantaged farmers and workers in developing countries receive a better deal for their products, decent working conditions, and fair terms of trade, as well as an additional Fairtrade Premium to invest in social or economic development projects.
Vegetarian Society ![Vegetarian Society APPROVED] Vegan Society ![Vegan]	Companies and shops do not have to label products as suitable for vegans or vegetarians, but some do. Some companies have their own symbols while others use the Vegetarian Society symbol or the Vegan Society symbol. The Vegetarian Society symbol is found on food products: • which are free of animal flesh or any product resulting from animal slaughter • which are free of ingredients which have been tested on animals • which are free of genetically modified ingredients • where eggs, if used, are free range. The Vegan Society symbol is found on food products which must, as far as is possible, be entirely free from any animal product. This label also indicates that during the development of the product there has been no animal testing.
Soil Association Organic Standard ![Soil Association Organic Standard]	This symbol is shown on foods which have been produced to strict animal welfare and environmental standards (especially relating to the use of fertilisers and pesticides).
GM Free	Genetic modification (GM) is the process of improving the characteristics of food ingredients and products by altering their genetic structures. The Soil Association symbol and the Vegetarian Society symbol are also guarantees of GM-free food. If a food is genetically modified, or has any ingredient included which is genetically modified, this must be stated on the food label.

Eco labelling of non-food products

BUAV	Companies approved under the British Union for the Abolition of Vivisection's **Humane Cosmetics Standard** or **Humane Household Products Standard** no longer conduct or commission animal testing on their products and adhere to a strict Fixed Cut-Off Date policy for ingredients throughout their supply chain. This is the only internationally recognised scheme that enables consumers to easily identify cruelty free products.
Flower	This European Union symbol allows consumers to recognise and choose products which have been made with care for the environment in mind. This is commonly found in products including: ● electrical appliances which achieve very good energy efficiency levels ● dishwashers and washing machines which use less water and detergent ● tissue papers made from recycled fibres or fibres from specially managed forests ● textiles where the use of dyes and chemicals is controlled.

For you to do

8 Next time you are in a supermarket, compare the prices of the following organic and non-organic foods, and see if organic is always more expensive:
- I litre of milk
- I kilogram of apples
- I kilogram of tomatoes
- 250g butter
- I kg chicken breast fillets.

9 Next time you are in a supermarket, look at the range of cosmetics and toiletries on display. Make a note of the different types of animal welfare labels and symbols found on different products.

Internet activity

10 Visit the Fairtrade Foundation website, and write a short article about one food product and one non-food product which are featured on the website. In your article you should try to indicate how Fairtrade benefits disadvantaged farmers and workers.

Links to this site and other websites relating to Standard Grade Home Economics can be found at:

LECKIE&LECKIE
Learning Lab

The microwave labelling system

As from 1992, all domestic microwave ovens have had to carry a new label, similar to the one detailed below. All food products which carry microwave-cooking instructions make reference to this labelling scheme.

- An 800 W oven will cook faster than a 500 W oven.
- If your oven is rated D it will heat up small portions of food faster than one rated B.

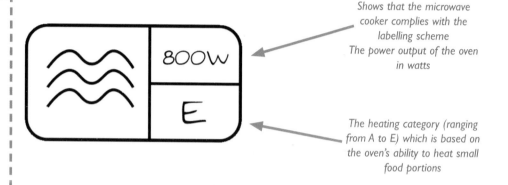

Shows that the microwave cooker complies with the labelling scheme
The power output of the oven in watts

The heating category (ranging from A to E) which is based on the oven's ability to heat small food portions

How it works

Packaged food that can be cooked in the microwave will be marked with the microwave symbol. The pack will also give instructions for heating using both the power rating and the heating category. Remember, food cooked or reheated in a microwave must always be piping hot.

For this product, you would cook the food for 4–5 minutes if your microwave cooker was an 800 W cooker or had a heat category of E.

If your microwave cooker had a heat category C, then you would cook the food for approximately 5–6 minutes.

TO MICROWAVE		HEAT ON FULL POWER	STAND
〰	800W E	2 1/2 MINUTES	1 MINUTE
〰	650W C	3 1/2 MINUTES	1 MINUTE

Labels on other products

The following labels can be seen on a variety of products.

BS en 71

In 1989 the British Toy and Hobby Association introduced the Lion Mark as a symbol of safety and quality designed to warn the British consumer against the pitfalls of buying faulty toys for their children. A toy carrying the Lion Mark on itself or its packaging is made by a reputable manufacturer who adheres to a strict code of practice. This ensures that the manufacturer's toys are made to the highest standards of safety in force in the UK and Europe (currently BS EN 71). Toys bought from an Approved Lion Mark Retailer indicate that all toys in that shop conform to the Lion Mark standard.

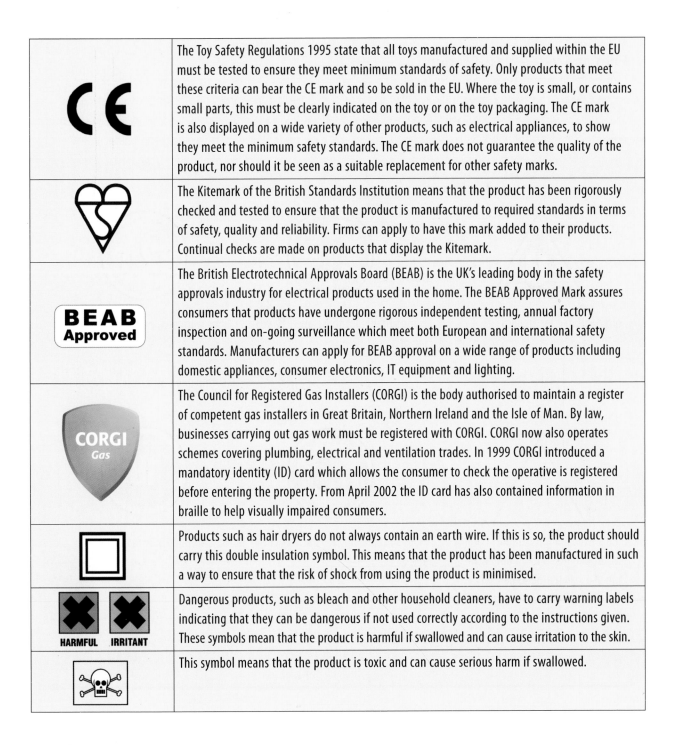

C E	The Toy Safety Regulations 1995 state that all toys manufactured and supplied within the EU must be tested to ensure they meet minimum standards of safety. Only products that meet these criteria can bear the CE mark and so be sold in the EU. Where the toy is small, or contains small parts, this must be clearly indicated on the toy or on the toy packaging. The CE mark is also displayed on a wide variety of other products, such as electrical appliances, to show they meet the minimum safety standards. The CE mark does not guarantee the quality of the product, nor should it be seen as a suitable replacement for other safety marks.
	The Kitemark of the British Standards Institution means that the product has been rigorously checked and tested to ensure that the product is manufactured to required standards in terms of safety, quality and reliability. Firms can apply to have this mark added to their products. Continual checks are made on products that display the Kitemark.
BEAB Approved	The British Electrotechnical Approvals Board (BEAB) is the UK's leading body in the safety approvals industry for electrical products used in the home. The BEAB Approved Mark assures consumers that products have undergone rigorous independent testing, annual factory inspection and on-going surveillance which meet both European and international safety standards. Manufacturers can apply for BEAB approval on a wide range of products including domestic appliances, consumer electronics, IT equipment and lighting.
CORGI *Gas*	The Council for Registered Gas Installers (CORGI) is the body authorised to maintain a register of competent gas installers in Great Britain, Northern Ireland and the Isle of Man. By law, businesses carrying out gas work must be registered with CORGI. CORGI now also operates schemes covering plumbing, electrical and ventilation trades. In 1999 CORGI introduced a mandatory identity (ID) card which allows the consumer to check the operative is registered before entering the property. From April 2002 the ID card has also contained information in braille to help visually impaired consumers.
	Products such as hair dryers do not always contain an earth wire. If this is so, the product should carry this double insulation symbol. This means that the product has been manufactured in such a way to ensure that the risk of shock from using the product is minimised.
HARMFUL IRRITANT	Dangerous products, such as bleach and other household cleaners, have to carry warning labels indicating that they can be dangerous if not used correctly according to the instructions given. These symbols mean that the product is harmful if swallowed and can cause irritation to the skin.
	This symbol means that the product is toxic and can cause serious harm if swallowed.

Film and video classification

During leisure activities many people like to watch videos and DVDs or go to the cinema. In order to ensure that young people, in particular, are not subjected to inappropriate scenes of violence or sex, there is an age-based classification system for film and videos. This rating system is also used for video and computer games.

Current classifications include:

Films suitable for all ages

Films suitable for those aged 12 years old or above

Films suitable for those aged 12 years old or above, but children under 12 years old are permitted if accompanied by a responsible adult

Films which might contain content unsuitable for children under the age of 15. Parental guidance is recommended before a child should watch this film

Films suitable only for those over the age of 15

Films suitable only for adults

GENERAL WELLBEING

There are a number of factors which combine together to ensure that we have good health:

- sleep
- a well-balanced diet
- fresh air and exercise
- personal cleanliness
- general good habits.

Some of these factors have been discussed fully in other sections. In this section we will look at sleep, exercise and general good habits.

Sleep

Our bodies need to rest. Even when we are resting and sleeping, our bodies are still functioning – our basic bodily functions still have to work. When we sleep, our bodily activities slow down so that the body can go to work repairing and replacing damaged cells. The amount of sleep that we need varies from person to person. However, the older we are, the less sleep we usually need. For example, babies sleep a great deal of the time whereas adults may need only six to eight hours per day. Other factors such as state of health, occupation and climate will also affect the amount of sleep that we require.

In order to get a good night's sleep there are some simple rules that you can follow.

- Try to wind down before going to bed. Working until late and then going straight to bed may result in a sleepless night.
- Try not to eat fatty or filling foods before going to bed. Your digestive system will have to work overtime to digest this food, and this can lead to poor sleep.
- A well-ventilated room will assist sleep.
- A warm bed also helps. If you are feeling tired and go into a cold bed, the end result might be that you feel wide-awake again!

Fresh air and exercise

Fresh air and exercise are good for the body. Not only do they help tone your muscles but they can help you to relax and sleep.

Fresh air is good for you as it ensures that the air you are breathing in is fresh and oxygen rich. This will help you to feel more alert.

Exercise in all forms, from running and swimming to dancing and playing golf, is good for the body:

- it gives you strength and vitality
- it helps you to sleep
- it can help you to reduce weight as you will burn up energy
- it improves stamina
- it tones the muscles and makes the heart, lungs and other muscles work more efficiently
- it can aid your appetite
- it can help you obtain good skin – through the action of moderate amounts of sunlight on the skin
- it can help to reduce stress.

Remember that if you are suffering from an illness it is important to seek medical attention before starting a vigorous exercise programme.

General good habits

By general good habits we mean looking after the body. The body can be particularly affected by the use of drugs. **Drugs** are chemicals that change the way a person's mind or body works and include:

- legal drugs (including medicines, alcohol, cigarettes, caffeine)
- illegal dugs (for example, heroin, crack, ecstasy)
- solvent abuse (using substances such as petrol or glue for their mind-altering effects).

Medicines are legal drugs. If you've ever been sick and had to take medicine you already know about this kind of drug. Medicines are legal drugs, meaning doctors are allowed to prescribe them for patients, chemists and supermarkets can sell them, and people are allowed to buy them. But it's not legal, or safe, for people to use these medicines any way they want or to buy them from people who are selling them illegally. Other legal drugs include alcohol and cigarettes – these are described on page 111–112.

Drug abuse

Drug abuse is the use of a drug for purposes for which it was not intended, or using a drug in excessive quantities. All sorts of different drugs can be abused, including illegal drugs such as heroin or cannabis, and legal drugs such as prescription drugs such as tranquillisers or painkillers, and other medicines that can be bought from the supermarket such as cough mixtures or herbal remedies. Some medications – for example, certain sleeping pills and painkillers – are addictive. They have an effect on the body which leads to **addiction,** and **withdrawal** symptoms may be experienced if the drug isn't taken. Others may lead to a psychological addiction if people have a craving for the effect that the drug gives.

All drugs carry risks.

- The effects may be unexpected, and will vary from person to person.
- Many drugs sold 'on the street' are mixed with other substances, so users can never be sure what they're getting.
- Users may become **tolerant** to some drugs (e.g. heroin and speed).
- Users may **overdose**. With heroin, an overdose can be fatal.
- Illegal drug use lead to arrest and a court appearance. Punishment may include a heavy fine, community service or a prison sentence.

Drug use can lead to very many different health problems including: becoming overheated, dehydrated, drowsy, faint or unconscious and contracting HIV and hepatitis B or C. Injecting can also damage veins.

In the UK, illegal drugs are classified into three main categories – A, B and C – some of which are listed below, along with current punishments (imprisonment and/or fine).

	CLASS A DRUGS	CLASS B	CLASS C
	Heroin Cocaine Crack Ecstasy LSD	Amphetamines (non-injection) Ice Barbiturates	Mild amphetamines Tranquillisers Anabolic steroids Cannabis
Maximum penalties - Possession - Supply	7 years+ fine Life imprisonment + fine	5 years + fine 14 years + fine	2 years + fine 14 years + fine

Drug: any natural or artificially made chemical which affects the way the mind or body function.
Addiction: the state of having a physical dependency on a drug for its effects, and not being able to stop.
Withdrawal: the period an addict goes through when not using drugs, often with extreme physical and mental symptoms.
Tolerant: this means the body has become so used to the drug the person needs to take more to get the same effect.
Overdose: too much of a drug taken or given at one time, either intentionally or by accident; can be fatal.

Solvent abuse

Solvent abuse includes the sniffing of gas and glue in order to get 'high' or get a 'buzz'. In the 10 years leading to 2004, there were 78 deaths in Scotland linked to substance abuse in Scotland. In the past, glue sniffing was a main cause of concern, but now glue sniffing has been replaced by abuse of aerosols, household products and gas lighter refills.

Sniffing solvents causes similar effects to those caused by alcohol. A sniffer can become drowsy, confused and aggressive. Half of those dying from solvent abuse die due to the direct effects of the chemicals that were sniffed while others die from the result of accidents, suffocation and choking on vomit. Death is often sudden and cardiac arrest is often a cause.

Alcohol

Current advice suggests that light consumption of alcohol can be good for the body. Some types of beer and wine contain chemicals that help in the fight against heart disease. When alcohol consumption is heavy it can lead to a variety of health-related problems. Excessive alcohol consumption can lead to dependency and this leads to addiction.

A person who experiences a strong desire to drink alcohol is known as an **alcoholic** – he or she suffers from **alcoholism**. If no alcohol is taken the sufferer experiences withdrawal symptoms which may include

shaking, sweating and nausea. Excess alcohol can lead to health problems including:

- depression
- liver cirrhosis (hardening and enlargement of the liver)
- heart failure.

It may also lead to family and other relationship breakdowns and possible problems at work.

How much is it safe to drink?

The **maximum** recommended amounts of drink that an individual should drink per week are:

- **Men** should drink no more than 21 units of alcohol per week (and no more than four units in any one day)
- **Women** should drink no more than 14 units of alcohol per week (and no more than three units in any one day)
- **Pregnant women** are advised not to drink in early pregnancy. If they have one or two drinks of alcohol (one or two units), once or twice a week, it is unlikely to harm the unborn baby. However, the exact amount that is safe is not known. So, many women have little or no alcohol when they are pregnant.

But what is a **unit**? As a rough guide:

- a very small glass of wine, a small glass of sherry, a single measure of spirit and a half-pint of beer each contain about **1 unit,** or 8g of alcohol
- a smallish 125ml glass of red or white wine or half a pint of cider contains about 1.5 units
- strong lager may contain as much as 2 units per half pint
- a 175ml glass of wine contains 2–2.5 units.
- a 500ml can/bottle of standard lager generally contains around 2.5 units
- a 750ml standard bottle of 12% wine contains around 9 units. Many wines are actually around 14.5%, which is nearly 11 units per bottle.

Smoker's lung: a condition with symptoms of frequent coughing, easily getting short of breath, and when the sputum is thick and difficult to cough up.
Passive smoking: the inhalation of smoke from other people.

Smoking

Smoking kills over 120,000 people in the UK each year. Cigarettes contain more than 4000 chemical compounds and at least 400 toxic substances. While the smoker is inhaling, a cigarette burns at 700°C at the tip and around 60°C in the core. This heat breaks down the tobacco to produce various poisons.

The products of cigarettes that are most damaging to health are tar (which can cause lung cancer), carbon monoxide and nicotine (which can cause heart and circulatory diseases), and other gases and tiny particles which cause **smoker's lung**. Other health hazards related to smoking include:

- coronary thrombosis (a blood clot in the arteries which can lead to heart disease)
- atherosclerosis (clogging up of the arteries which can lead to a stroke)
- high blood pressure
- kidney failure
- cancer – not only of the lung but also of the oesophagus, the kidneys, the pancreas, the cervix and the bladder
- bad breath, stained teeth and a strong smell of cigarette smoke.

Research has shown that smoking reduces life expectancy by 7–8 years. However, if a smoker gives up smoking at any stage, the rates of decline in lung capacity are reduced and this in turn postpones disability and handicap.

On the 26 March 2006 the Scottish Executive introduced a smoking ban in Scotland. The Prohibition of Smoking in Certain Premises (Scotland) Regulations 2006 were designed to protect the public from the harmful effects of **passive smoking**. There is scientific evidence to show that people who do not smoke but who socialise or work in the company of people who do smoke, are likely to inhale smoke and so suffer health problems. (Secondary smoke is actually more toxic than smoke inhaled by the smoker.) The law makes it an offence to smoke in any enclosed public place, for example, the workplace, football stadiums, bars and restaurants.

Many of the large supermarkets, such as ASDA, are raising the age for buying cigarettes from 16 to 18. This decision was taken due to the concerns about the effect of smoking on health and to discourage young people from smoking. There is also debate in both Scotland and the UK as to whether the legal age for cigarette buying should be increased from 16 to 18.

For you to do

11 a What do you think are the benefits of the non-smoking ban to: restaurant workers; the general public; restaurant owners?
b Why do you think some people may be against this ban?

Quick Quiz

Select the correct answer **a**, **b**, **c** or **d** for each of the questions below.

1 Why does a policeman who is directing traffic wear a fluorescent jacket?
  a Because it is fashionable
  b To be seen clearly/to be visible
  c To keep him warm
  d To keep his handcuffs safe

2 What is Velcro?
  a A special type of fastening
  b A baby food
  c A type of shoe
  d An item of baby clothing

3 Which of the following design features would be important in the clothing of a pregnant woman?
  a Zipper pocket
  b Designer logo
  c Elasticated waistband on trousers
  d Tight-fitting design

4 Which of the following does NOT assist with clothing insulation?
  a Quilting
  b Layering
  c Stain resistance
  d Wool as a main fibre content

5 What does the following symbol tell us?

  a The item is safe to use
  b The item meets flammability safety tests
  c The item used recycled materials
  d The item does not meet flammability tests

6 What does the abbreviation CAB stand for?
  a Complaint Advice Bureau
  b Consumer Advice Bureau
  c Citizens Advice Bureau
  d Central American Bank

7 A consumer buys a new flat screen TV in a sale. It does not work when taken from the box and used. To what is the consumer entitled?
  a Nothing
  b Only a repair
  c Only an exchange
  d A refund

8 Which of the following does not have to appear on a food label?
  a Indication of shelf life
  b Picture or illustration of the product
  c Product weight
  d Storage instructions

9

TO MICROWAVE	HEAT ON FULL POWER	STAND
800W E	2 1/2 MINUTES	1 MINUTE
650W C	3 1/2 MINUTES	1 MINUTE

This symbol appears on a food package. What is the total cooking time for the product if using an 800 W oven?
  a 4 minutes
  b 3½ minutes
  c 2½ minutes
  d 8 minutes

10 You are looking for a qualified gas installer to fit a new gas fire. Which of the following symbols would you look for to ensure you were using a qualified gas installer?

a
b CORGI Gas
c BEAB Approved
d BS en 71

CHAPTER 8: MANAGEMENT OF EXPENDITURE

In this chapter

- Budgeting
- Sources of income
- Household expenditure
- Purchasing goods and services
- Debt management

BUDGETING

Budgeting is about **balancing** the amount of money that comes into a house with the amount being spent. The ideal position to be in is to have a small amount of money left over each month that can be **saved**. Balancing the budget is what a household should be aiming for. If a household is constantly spending more money than is coming in, then the household will end up in **debt**.

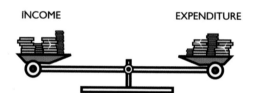

SOURCES OF INCOME

We can classify income according to whether it is:

 fixed – usually remains the same from month to month

or

 variable – changes from month to month.

When planning a budget it is better to rely on fixed income which is guaranteed and reliable.

 If a person is employed, they will earn an **income**, either a wage or a salary, depending on the job. People earning a **wage** tend to be paid a fixed rate for each hour worked. This is then paid to the worker at the end of each week. This may be paid in cash but more likely it will be paid directly into a bank account. A person earning a **salary** will be paid a fixed amount each year and this will usually be paid in 12 monthly instalments. This is most likely to be paid directly into a bank account.

No matter how you get paid, you will get a **wage slip**. This details how much money you have earned. The wage slip will also show what **deductions** have been made. These deductions will be:

- **Income tax:** Everybody who earns above a certain amount of money has to pay income tax to the government.
- **National insurance:** Every person who earns above a certain amount of money has to pay national insurance to the government.
- **Pension payments**: Some companies operate a pension scheme for employees. If you have agreed to enter one of these schemes (also called superannuation schemes) money will be deducted from your earnings.

The money you get paid before your deductions is called your **gross income**. The money you get paid after your deductions is called your **net income**:

NET INCOME = GROSS INCOME − DEDUCTIONS

Other sources of income

	Pensions: Some people may be entitled to a state or private pension. When you retire you are entitled to a state pension. The government pays money direct to you. People who have set up a private pension fund will be paid an additional amount from this fund.
	Interest: If you have a savings account or a current account that pays interest you will receive interest on a monthly basis. This amount of money will vary depending on what you are saving.
	Dividends: Some people buy shares in companies. The companies pay out dividends (similar to interest payments) regularly. The amount paid out varies considerably.
	Benefits/Tax credits: People who are on low incomes, who are unemployed, who are too ill to work or who meet other specified criteria (such as having children) will be paid money by the government. The amount varies depending on what benefit they are on and how much money they have saved.

HOUSEHOLD EXPENDITURE

As well as classifying expenditure according to whether it is fixed or variable, we can also classify it according to whether it is:

 essential – a type of expenditure that we must pay

or

 non-essential – a type of expenditure that we could do without.

The table on pages 116–117 summarises the main areas of personal, family and household expenditure.

EXPENDITURE AREA	FIXED OR VARIABLE	ESSENTIAL OR NON-ESSENTIAL	COMMENTS
Food	V	E	We need food to survive. Food can provide us with the correct balance of nutrients, depending on the choices we make. Food bills vary with the family size and the age and sex of the people in the house. Some food costs can be reduced through shopping around and avoiding unnecessary waste but savings can be made from other areas first. (Recent figures indicate that UK households waste/throw away about one-third of all the food they buy.)
Clothing	V	E	We need clothing for warmth and protection from the elements. The amount of money spent on clothing will vary depending on the age and sex of the people in the household. Some savings can be made in this area but only after non-essential areas have been reduced.
Shelter	V	E	We need shelter to protect us and keep us safe and secure. This part of the budget normally includes rent or mortgage payments. This is an area where it is difficult to make any savings. If you do not make these payments you may not have a home to stay in.
Maintenance of shelter	V	E	This includes general maintenance costs, household cleaning, and repairs. It is important that you make any necessary repairs to your home, including general maintenance and cleaning. If housing repairs are not undertaken, then the damage may get worse and then be more expensive to fix. Certain savings can be made in this area but not before all of the non-essential areas have been reduced.
Fuel	V	E	We need fuel to ensure that our houses remain warm and that we can cook food. The amount of fuel that we use will vary depending on the time of year. Most companies offer a monthly payment scheme – they estimate your fuel costs for the year and you pay this in instalments. This can help with budgeting. You can now get your gas and electricity from the same supplier and they will usually give you a discount for this. You can make some savings in this area (see pages 76–77 for advice and tips to save energy) but not before you have reduced spending in non-essential areas.
Taxes/ Insurance	F	E	There are a number of taxes that you must pay. Income tax and National insurance are automatically deducted from your pay. You will also have to pay Council tax. If you have insurance policies it is advisable to keep up with these payments as in the longer term, they may help you avoid bigger costs.
Transport	V	E or N	This section depends on your circumstances. If you rely on transport for getting to and from work then this area is essential. If, however, you could walk or cycle to work then this area may be less essential. Transport costs include the costs of motoring (e.g. road tax, MOT, car insurance, all of which you must have by law). Petrol costs and car maintenance will also be included here.

Debit and credit agreements	**F**	**E**	If you have any hire purchase agreements it is advisable to keep up with these payments, otherwise the goods may be taken from you. It is always advisable to make your credit payments on a regular basis. If you are experiencing problems, however, there are further steps that you can take. See pages 124 – 125 for more information.
Personal purchases	**V**	**F**	This category includes purchases that might be considered as non-essential or luxury items such as aftershave and perfume, cigarettes, alcohol, magazines, CDs and DVDs, computer games, etc. It would also include pets and pet food. These are items that we can normally do without if we need to save money.
Savings	**V**	**F**	It is good to have money to put aside for a 'rainy day'. It may not be possible to do so – particularly if you are finding it difficult to make ends meet.
Entertainment/ Sport/Leisure	**V**	**F**	This includes areas such as the cinema, theatre, bingo, going to pubs and nightclubs, as well as expenditure on sports such as football matches, golf, horse-riding. This category is where you can reduce expenditure.
Travel and holidays	**V**	**F**	This is another category where you can reduce expenditure. Holiday-related costs include spending money, travel insurance and possibly new clothes.

Identifying priorities

It is important to remember that everybody has different sets of priorities. Those sections marked as essential are the main priorities that have to be considered when making a household budget. The areas marked as non-essential are the areas that can be easily reduced. We must also consider individuals' beliefs, values and preferences when developing a household budget. Here are two specific examples to explain this:

- Household A is a very religious family. They set aside 10% of their net income for their church or temple. This would be reflected in the budget for this household.
- Household B consists of an elderly man living alone. He has a pet dog. For this household, the dog is an important consideration as it provides companionship, and encourages the man to go walking. The importance of the pet to the man's life makes it essential expenditure, and this would be reflected in the budget for this household.

If, when the household budget is planned, there is an **excess of income over expenditure**, this excess can be budgeted as **savings**. If, however, there is an **excess of expenditure over income**, then savings will have to be made in the non-essential categories in order to get the budget to **balance** and avoid **debt**.

HINTS & TIPS

As shown in the example of the elderly man above, whether an item of expenditure is essential or non-essential will sometimes depend on the circumstances of the individual. Questions in an exam may ask you to identify priorities in different situations. You need to consider these carefully when identifying whether expenditure is essential or non-essential.

For you to do

I Read the following case study and answer the question that follows.

Ramir and Faza are a newly married couple. They have a steady monthly income of £2500. Their monthly expenditure is shown in the table. Ramir and Faza have £1500 of savings. Ramir has recently been made unemployed and the couple need to review and amend their budget. Faza is still working. Their income will reduce by £1000 per month. Ramir and Faza did not pay their mortgage last month.

ITEM	EXPENDITURE	ITEM	EXPENDITURE
Mortgage	£700	Saving for holidays	£150
Insurances	£250	Gym membership	£90
Council tax	£180	Car expenses	£250
Fuel for heating	£60	Clothing	£300
Food	£375	Magazines	£45
Savings	£100	**Total expenditure**	**£2500**

What advice can you provide Ramir and Faza with regard to their budget and their mortgage arrears (the mortgage amount they have not paid)?

PURCHASING GOODS AND SERVICES

There are many ways to pay for goods and services. The methods that people use will depend on the circumstances of the purchase and the personal circumstances and needs of the individuals.

Main methods of payment

METHOD OF PAYMENT	COMMENTS
Cash	The easiest and most straightforward method of payment. You can only buy what you have available to spend. If you carry large amounts of money, there is a possible danger of theft or loss of money.
Electronic funds transfer at point of sale (EFTPOS)	Specific examples include Switch, Delta and Visa Electron cards. Anybody who has a suitable bank account can have an EFTPOS facility. This means they are given a debit card (a cash card) which allows them to pay for goods using the card. This plastic card stores their account details on a magnetic strip or microchip. When the card is swiped through the shop till, their bank account is instantly debited. With this method they can usually only spend up to the balance that is in their bank account. Debit cards are now Chip and PIN cards.

Personal cheque and Cheque card	Available to customers who hold a bank current account. Normally, the bank provides the customer with a cheque card, which acts as a guarantee to the shopkeeper that the bank will honour (pay) any cheque the customer writes, up to the limit indicated on the cheque card. When using this method, you write out a cheque detailing the amount of money to be paid to the payee in exchange for goods or services. The payee pays the cheque into their account, and it is transferred through the banking system to your bank, at which time the cheque amount is deducted from your account (a few days later). This is a convenient method of paying for goods, but it is important to keep track of all the cheques you have written so you always have enough money in your bank account to cover the amounts you have spent. If you don't have enough, you will be contacted by the bank and may be charged a fee for over-spending on your account. Increasingly, many shops are no longer accepting cheques for payment of goods and services.
Credit card	For example, Visa and Mastercard. Usually only available to people who have a regular income and satisfy other requirements. Each customer is given a credit limit. Purchases can be made up to this limit. Each customer is given a plastic credit card, which holds their account details on a magnetic strip or microchip. The card is usually swiped through the till and the machine records their purchase details. Every month they are sent a statement showing the purchases they have made. This purchase balance can either be paid in full, or a portion of the sum can be paid. If the entire balance is not paid, they are charged interest on the balance remaining. With this method of payment, it is very easy to get carried away and spend more than you can afford. Some credit card companies now charge an annual fee. Most credit cards are now Chip and PIN cards.
Charge card	For example, American Express. This works in a similar manner to a credit card, except that you have to pay the balance in full at the end of each month. Again, the charge card company may charge an annual fee. Most charge cards are now Chip and PIN cards.

Chip and PIN cards

In May 2003, **Chip and PIN** cards were introduced into the UK. Where a shop accepts debit, credit or charge cards it will carry the Chip and PIN logo – as shown below.

Chip and PIN is the new, more secure way to pay with credit, debit or charge cards in the UK. Instead of using your signature to verify payments, you are asked to enter a four digit Personal Identification Number (PIN) known only to you.

Chip and **PIN**

For you to do

2 Why do you think that the UK banks introduced Chip and PIN?
    If you want more information about Chip and PIN, visit the Chip and PIN website.

Links to this site and other websites relating to Standard Grade Home Economics can be found at:

Deferred payment systems

Some methods of payment let you defer payment, that is, put off payment or spread it out over a longer period of time.

METHOD OF PAYMENT	COMMENTS
Credit sale agreement	This is only available from certain stores and only for those customers who meet certain criteria (i.e. those able to make repayments). A down-payment is usually paid towards the cost of the items to be purchased. The balance is then paid in fixed monthly payments over several months. Some companies offer interest-free agreements. You own the goods immediately.
Hire purchase (HP)	Similar to credit sale agreement, but more likely to be used for purchasing larger items such as cars. Interest is normally charged with HP agreements. You don't own the goods until the final payment is made, and if you fall behind with your HP payments, the goods can be taken from you.
Store budget account	This is only available from certain stores and only to those customers who meet certain criteria. It works in the same way as a credit card, but you are limited as to where the card can be used. Consumers are given a credit limit from a particular store or groups of stores. Regular payments are made each month, and it is the amount of payment that is made that determines your credit limit. Interest is payable on outstanding balances. Interest charges can sometimes be quite high.
Store charge account	This works like a credit card, but you can only use it in certain stores. Interest is payable on outstanding balances. Your credit limit is set at the start of the agreement and is not based on how much you pay monthly. Interest charges can sometimes be quite high.

By law, all companies offering credit have to display the **annual percentage rate** of interest (APR) they charge. APR allows customers to compare different rates of credit. The higher the APR, the more expensive the credit will be.

Credit, debit, and charge cards can be stolen and used **fraudulently** by other people. Stolen cards should always be reported to the police.

Many banks now offer customers **smart cards**. These are credit, debit and cash machine cards all in one. These allow you to access money from a cash machine 24 hours a day.

You have to be 18 years old to obtain credit.

WORD BANK

Defer: to delay something (e.g. payment) until later.

Annual percentage rate (APR): a method of calculating interest over 1 year.

Credit history: a database recording your financial transactions over a period of time, showing how well you have managed your finances.

Fraudulent: dishonest.

Before offering you credit, companies will contact Credit Reference Agencies to check on your **credit history**. If you have had debt problems, you may find it difficult to obtain credit.

> **How much can credit cost?**
> Yvonne decides to buy a printer. She has a choice of paying by cash or using her credit card.
> If she pays cash, the printer will cost **£350.00**.
> If she pays using her credit card and takes a year to pay it off, she will have to pay interest of 13.9%* or **£48.65**. So the total cost of the printer, including credit charges, would be **£398.65**.
> ***Note**: this rate is only an example; APR can vary considerably from 0% to over 30%.

Advantages and disadvantages of buying goods by cash

ADVANTAGES	DISADVANTAGES
● You can only buy what you can afford – you will not get into debt. ● It is an easy and convenient way to pay for goods and services.	● It can be dangerous to carry large amounts of cash. ● You can lose money by accident. ● It can be difficult to purchase items which are on special offer or reduced price if you are limited in the funds you have available.

Advantages and disadvantages of buying goods on credit

ADVANTAGES	DISADVANTAGES
● It saves having to carry large amounts of cash around. ● Used wisely, it can give you interest-free credit. ● It can be used for emergencies or for picking up sale bargains. ● You may gain additional protection if you purchase items on credit (e.g. if you purchase an expensive item which proves to be faulty and the shop where you purchased it has closed down, you can make a claim from the credit provider). ● You can use credit and charge cards to obtain cash from cash machines. (However, some banks will charge you for making a withdrawal.)	● You usually have to pay interest and so items cost more. ● There are criteria that you have to meet before you can obtain credit. ● It is easy to overspend and have problems repaying the debt. ● Certain types of credit (e.g. credit and store cards) can be used fraudulently if lost or stolen. ● Certain types of credit are not available for use in every store.

Getting value for money

Whatever method of purchase you use, it always pays to shop around when buying goods and services, to ensure that you are getting the best value for your money.

Buying goods and services

- Look around different shops and stores to see the range available and to check and compare prices.
- Use the internet, mail order and TV shopping in order to compare prices of products.
- Use *Which*? magazine to get an idea of what is considered the 'best buy'.
- Ask friends or relatives for advice and information.
- Shop assistants can provide useful information, but remember that such information may not always be reliable or objective.

Shopping for groceries

- Buying in bulk from a cash and carry or supermarket may work out cheaper in the long term.
- Discount supermarkets stock less well known brands of foods, but they are usually less expensive.
- Supermarkets' own brand products can often be cheaper than well known brand names.
- Make use of special offers if appropriate (e.g. buy two, get one free).
- Money-off vouchers can help to reduce shopping bills. Even if you can't use them when shopping for food this week, keep them until you can.
- Some products (e.g. bread) are sold at a reduced price at the end of the shopping day.
- Some companies now offer free delivery and internet food ordering.
- Local corner shops tend to be more expensive than supermarkets. However, they do sometimes have special offers and so shopping around can be useful.

Shopping for credit

- Investigate and compare different lenders to get the best deal.
- Read the small print carefully.
- Think carefully about whether you will still be able to afford the repayments in a few months' time.
- Check the APR rates as well as other conditions (e.g. initial deposit to be paid, the period of repayment, and what happens if you miss payments).

For you to do

3 Moyra is planning to buy a new mobile phone and has the option of paying for the phone by cash or by spreading the amount over 12 months and paying by **direct debit**. The APR for this agreement will be 0%. What are the advantages to Moyra of each method of payment?

Direct debit: an agreement where you sign a form authorising your bank to pay an agreed amount of money into another's bank account (person, shop or service provider) every month.

Internet shopping

More and more consumers are using their computers to buy things like software,
CDs and books, as well as some services. Like mail order, people appreciate the
convenience of not having to walk around the shops, and can browse among a
huge choice of goods in their own time. Your rights when buying over the internet
are the same as when you buy goods from the high street. However, there are
some safety and security aspects you should know about.

Shopping online

1 Be careful when you give your credit or
debit card details on the internet. Always
find out whether the company has a secure

site by looking for the closed padlock sign
at the bottom of the screen, and look
for information about the protection the
company has put in place.

2 As with any other type of purchase, shop
around for the best deals and prices. In most
cases, you are entitled to a seven working day
cancellation period where you can change
your mind, but this usually does not apply to
'auction' sites, for example, eBay.

3 Watch out for high postage rates and for
other hidden costs, such as VAT and other
duty payable, particularly if goods are being
sent from abroad.

4 There are logos that indicate that you
are shopping on a secure weblink. Some
companies, including Comet, use this logo:

5 If you are buying items from overseas,
remember that if you have problems such
as faulty goods or non-delivery, it might be
very difficult to get your complaint dealt
with. Although your contract will probably be
covered by UK law – allowing you to sue in
your local court – it may be difficult to get
money out of a company based abroad.

6 Most importantly, print out the order, and
keep any terms and conditions that appear
on the website, just in case of any disputes or
problems later on.

Savings schemes

There are many different types of savings schemes other than those available from regular banks, building societies and credit unions.

Many supermarkets offer regular saving schemes for Christmas, where you buy stamps or place money on to a plastic savings card which you can then spend in the period leading up to Christmas. Many of these schemes are safe, but such schemes tend to be unregulated, which can cause problems if things go wrong. One particular scheme that went wrong late in 2006 was the Farepak scheme.

Farepak collected monthly amounts of money from clients, and issued vouchers that the clients could use at specified retailers. It relied on the retailers waiting until after Christmas for bills to be settled. However, Farepak's bank changed some of their financial arrangements, which Farepak were unable to meet. Despite uncertainty about the scheme, savers were assured that their money was safe and so continued to make payments into the scheme. Eventually the scheme collapsed late in 2006. Savers received only 4p for every pound saved, meaning they lost an average of £400 each, although some lost nearly £2000.

The government called for an inquiry into the Farepak situation. And as a result of the Farepak disaster, all Christmas saving clubs are now regulated.

For you to do

4 Rather than saving money by such schemes, how else could a consumer save money for Christmas?

DEBT MANAGEMENT

When debt occurs, it can be a time of great worry and stress. If the debt is small, you may be able to adjust your household budget by reducing your expenditure on non-essential items. However, if the debt is getting out of control, you need to take a variety of steps.

1 Do not take on any further debt – this will only make your present situation worse.

2 Do not transfer debt from one credit card to another credit card or pay debt using a credit card.

3 Do not ignore letters and phone calls from your **creditors** (the people that you owe money to). The problem will not go away.

4 Contact all your creditors and let them know of your current financial difficulties. They may be able to assist you by extending the repayment period or reducing your monthly payments.

5 Keep records of all telephone calls made and copies of all correspondence.

6 Make a detailed note of your entire monthly income and expenditure. The credit companies may request that you send them this information before they can assist you. It will also let you have a clearer picture of what your financial situation is. It is important that your income and expenditure sheet is accurate and reliable.

7 If you are having real financial difficulties there is help and advice available from a range of sources, such as those below.

Citizens Advice Bureau

Citizens Advice Bureaus (CABs) have specially trained advisers who can give you free help and advice to help resolve your debt problems. They will be able to help you draw up a debt management plan, based on your income and expenditure. The address and telephone number of the local CAB can be found in the telephone directory. See page 96 for more information on CABs.

Consumer Advice Centre

These centres offer practical help and advice on a variety of shopping-related matters. Staff are trained to offer free and confidential advice – including advice on debt management. See page 96 for more information on CACs.

Credit union

Credit unions are set up in local communities to offer financial services to local people. They have trained staff who deal with money management issues and will be able to provide help and assistance. They may be able to refer you to another appropriate organisation for additional help and support.

Company, bank, building society

It is important to contact the people (for example, company, bank or building society) that you owe money to. When they are aware of your financial difficulties they will be able to work with you to help resolve your problems. Most credit-lending bodies offer free advice and will be able to assist consumers in this situation.

Other sources of help

Some companies advertise in the media, offering a service to assist consumers that have financial difficulties. They offer a package of measures to reduce your monthly credit repayments. (They do not offer a loan – they simply deal with all your creditors and try to agree a reduced payment programme.) It is important to remember that these companies may charge you a monthly fee that you could be using to pay off your existing debt.

The Consumer Credit Counselling Service (CCCS) offers you a similar service, which is free. This service has the backing of most credit companies. You can find the telephone number of the CCCS in the telephone book.

Internet activity

5 Jamie is a member of a credit union, and he wants to borrow £800. He plans to pay the money back in 15 monthly instalments, and wishes to know how much this would cost him so that he can work out his budget carefully. To see how this can be worked out, go to the Drumchapel Community Credit Union website, and click on the loans calculator icon on the left-hand side of the screen.
   a How much will each repayment be?
   b How much will the total repayment be?
   c How much interest will he pay?
Links to this site and other websites relating to Standard Grade Home Economics can be found at: **LECKIE&LECKIE Learning Lab**

Quick Quiz

Answer true or false.
1 Food is a non-essential item of expenditure.
2 Taxes are a variable item of expenditure.
3 A person in debt should not pay expenses for shelter.
4 A person in debt should contact their creditors immediately.
5 Entertainment is an essential item of expenditure.
6 APR stands for Annual Percentage Rate.
7 A debit card is a form of credit card.
8 To get a credit card you have to be over the age of 18.
9 Anybody can get hire purchase or a loan.
10 A credit union is a company used by a credit company to check your credit history.

ANSWERS

Chapter 1: Eating a variety of foods contributes to good health

Activities

1 Milk: protein, fat, calcium, vitamins A, B1, B2, D and K, phosphorus, carbohydrate; baked potato: carbohydrate, vitamin C; cheese: protein, fat, calcium, phosphorus, vitamins A and D, sodium; apple: vitamin C.

2 **a** Protein, carbohydrate, fat, vitamin B
   b Iron, vitamin C, vitamin K, folic acid

3 Chart input (order from left to right, row by row):
   row 1: disaccharides; **row 2:** galactose, maltose, non-starch polysaccharides; **row 3:** honey/fruit/vegetables; sugar cane/sugar beet/vegetables

4 **a** Stir-fried red meat, peppers, cabbage and green vegetables is a good combination because the peppers, cabbage and green vegetables will be a source of vitamin C which will help to absorb the iron from the red meat.
   b Pasta dish containing a cheddar cheese sauce and spinach is a poor combination as spinach contains oxalic acid which will prevent some of the absorption of calcium from the cheese and milk. Cheese contains some saturated fat which may also reduce absorption of calcium.

Quick Quiz

1 false	**2** true	**3** true	**4** true	**5** true
6 true	**7** false	**8** true	**9** false	**10** true

Chapter 2: Current dietary advice

Activities

1 **a** Scotland has not been successful in achieving the Scottish dietary targets. In fact, progress towards achievement of the targets in some cases may be worse now than when the targets were first developed:
   ● fruit and vegetable target – no progress
   ● we are eating more sugar that when target was set
   ● we are eating fewer potatoes than when target was set
   ● we are eating less brown and wholemeal bread than when targets set.
   b The main reasons for lack of success include:
   ● promotion needs a stronger focus on key aims
   ● promotion needs to be on a larger scale
   ● inadequate resources and initiatives to promote/integrate the targets
   ● competitive advertising of less healthy foods.

3

ORIGINAL INGREDIENT	CHANGE TO
margarine	low fat spread/vegetable oil/olive oil
plain flour	wholemeal flour
full cream milk	semi or skimmed milk
cheddar cheese	low fat cheddar cheese
small pinch salt	low salt alternative or omit altogether

4 **a** Christopher's BMI is 20.0; Ryan's BMI is 28.9.
   b Christopher's BMI is good, showing he is a healthy weight for his age and height. Ryan's BMI is not as good, and suggests he may be overweight, given his age and height.

8 **a** Pasta **b** Pasta **c** Pasta **d** Pizza
   e 458 calories **f** 916 calories **g** 1.6 g

Quick Quiz

1 true	**2** true	**3** true	**4** true	**5** false
6 true	**7** false	**8** true	**9** false	**10** true

Chapter 3: Individuals have varying dietary needs

Activities

1 **a** Boys require more energy because
   (i) they tend to be more active than girls, and
   (ii) they tend to be bigger, and have larger body frames.
   b Teenage girls require more iron than teenage boys due to menstrual blood loss.
   c As women age, they tend to become less active and so their energy needs reduce.
   d As both men and women age, protein is needed only for maintenance and repair of tissues and not for growth, so needs are reduced.

2

1 C	**2** B	**3** A	**4** F	**5** E
6 D	**7** G	**8** I	**9** J	**10** H

3 Examples include:
   ● the Atkins diet, which excludes all carbohydrates in the diet. This can be bad for health in the long term as you are increasing your saturated fat intake and excluding a major food group in your diet.

   ● the Cabbage soup diet, in which the main component is cabbage soup, although other combinations are allowed. This can be bad for heath as there is little energy content in the food consumed and so you can tire quickly. If followed for a long time, this diet can leave you deficient in many important nutrients.
   Note: all 'fad' diets can cause health risks and medical advice should be sought before starting.

4

1 R,C	**2** M	**3** H	**4** H	**5** I
6 H	**7** M	**8** P	**9** M	**10** R,C

Quick Quiz

1 Reference Nutrient Intake
2 False
3 This is time of increased body growth
4 Iron and vitamin C
5 Liver, pate, raw eggs, undercooked eggs, soft cheeses, cook chill foods, foods containing raw eggs
6 Fish, meat and animal flesh (but does eat eggs).
7 Hinduism, Buddhism
8 A plant-based protein food commonly eaten by vegetarians
9 False
10 False

Chapter 4: Cleanliness is important in relation to health

Activities

1 The International Care Labelling System allows consumers to understand the washing instructions for foreign and imported clothing, enabling them to care correctly for clothing regardless of the language at the point of manufacture.

2 Product: must be dry cleaned only; must not be washed; must not be bleached; must not be tumble-dried; can be ironed using a cool iron.

3 To ensure that the employee has read and understands basic food safety rules. To protect the employer as they can claim that the staff member has read/understood the rules because they have signed the document.

5 Jams include raspberry, strawberry, blackcurrant, mixed fruit, apricot. Marmalades include orange, lime, grapefruit.

6 **a** Freezer burn: a type of food spoilage cause by incorrect packaging of food in a domestic freezer. Where a food surface is exposed to severely cold temperatures water evaporates from the surface of the food causing it to dehydrate.

b Quick-freeze: the rapid freezing of foods in a domestic freezer at temperatures of about $-22°C$. This drop in temperature allows food to freeze more quickly, minimising damage to the cellular structure of the food, so when the food is defrosted, its texture is better.

c Tetra Pak: a special type of packaging used to package and store food, mainly liquids, e.g. milk, fruit juices, soups.

7 Wordsearch answers: vomiting; use by; eighty two; defrost; three; carrier; doctor

8 The temperature of the fridge should be between $0°C$ and $4°C$. If the temperature is above this the fridge is not working efficiently/effectively and so food spoilage/deterioration may be speeded up.

Quick Quiz

1 $82°C$ 2 $4°C$

3 Pre-frozen foods can be stored for a maximum of 3 months from purchase.

4 $63°C$ 5 Between $-18°C$ and $-22°C$

6 Symptoms include: severe vomiting; diarrhoea; exhaustion; headache; fever; abdominal pain; tiredness.

7 Perishable foods   8 Top shelf

9 Personal hygiene concerns the person handling the food; kitchen hygiene concerns the environment in which it is prepared

Chapter 5: Safe working practices

Activities

1

SAFETY HAZARD	PREVENTION
Father pulling electrical cord from socket – possible electric shock	Pull electrical plugs from sockets using hands, ensuring hands are dry and that the power source for the socket is switched off.
Power sockets overloaded– possible electric shock or fire risk	Remove most of the appliances from the socket and plug into other power sources. Use an extension lead if required but do not overload with appliances.
Too strong a bulb in the lamp – risk of overheating and possible fire	Change bulb to a lower wattage (preferably using an energy saving bulb).
Toy lying on floor – possible trip	Do not leave toys lying about – place in a cupboard/toy box.
Electric fire without guard – possible burn	Switch electric fire off if possible when toddler is in the room. Place a fire-guard around the electric fire to prevent the toddler getting burnt.
Cup of hot tea on the table – possible scald	Do not leave hot liquids in places where a toddler can access them.
Electric flex on lamp has been taped – possible electric shock	A qualified electrician should be employed to replace the electric flex on the lamp.
Trailing flex on lamp – possible fall	Try to locate the lamp near a socket to prevent the flex from trailing. Place the flex behind the couch to prevent people tripping over it.

2 **a** Approximately 3000

b Carry out safety audits in the home; provide safety information and advice to consumers

c Home Safety Response Team, Home Safety Officer or Home Safety Adviser

Quick Quiz

1 C   2 B   3 C   4 A, C   5 B
6 B   7 C   8 A   9 A   10 A

Chapter 6: Design features

Activities

3 **a** Polyester and nylon   **b** Wool   **c** Wool

d It is not durable and so may not survive the extremes of outdoor use; it does not provide warmth that would be required from an outdoor jacket.

5 **a** Washing machine   **b** B

c Yes, but not the best. It is the second-top rating.

d A   **e** B

f Washing machines can be noisy; if you want one that is quiet when operating then the noise information would be useful.

g You would look at the information about water consumption. The higher the number the greater the water use and so the more you would have to pay the water company.

6 **a** garden waste 21%, textiles 3%; plastics, 7% in total
b garden waste
c 40 years ago disposable nappies were not available

Quick Quiz
1 A = 2, 4, 5, 7   B = 6   C = 3   D = 1   E = 5, 2
2 1 C   2 D   3 E   4 B   5 A

Chapter 7: Physical needs of individuals and families

Activities
1 The running jacket may include the following design features (the list is not exhaustive): fluorescent strips – to be seen at night/when dark; pockets – to keep keys/torch safe and secure; lightweight – to allow him to run without carrying additional weight; showerproof/rainproof – to keep him dry when running; drawcord at waist – to prevent draughts/ prevent drag when running; breathable membranes – to allow sweat out and so maintain comfort when running.

2 The training shoe may include the following design features (the list is not exhaustive) reflective strips for road running safety; anti-microbial treatment to prevent growth of odour causing microbes; impact pads that help protect feet when running; Velcro closing trainers; no lace up trainers; specially designed soles to enhance grip on surface.

3 Benefits; debt; employment; housing; legal

6 You are entitled to a refund.

7 **a** CAB, EHO, CAC; Food Safety Act
b CAB, Trading Standards, CAC; Trade Descriptions Act, Sale of Goods Act
c CAB, EHO   **d** CA
e Trading Standards, CAB, CAC
f CAB, CAC, Trading Standards; Sale of Goods Act
g EHO, FSA

11 **a** Restaurant workers: reduction in passive smoking intake; no cigarette smoke on clothing or body at end of work; no cigarette ash/stubs/ashtrays to clean at end of work. General public: reduction in passive smoking intake; no cigarette smoke on clothing or body when in pubs and other enclosed public spaces; cleaner atmosphere/environment; can eat in bars and restaurants without having to inhale smoke. Restaurant owners: encourages families into restaurants; healthier for staff working in restaurant.
b Against the ban: smokers do not like the inconvenience of having to go outside to smoke; bar owners etc. may see a reduction in trade especially from smokers; smokers see this ban as affecting their human right to smoke.

Quick Quiz
1 B   **2** A   **3** C   **4** C   **5** B
6 C   **7** D   **8** B   **9** C   **10** B

Chapter 8: Management of expenditure

Activities
1 Advice for Ramir and Faza:
● The mortgage arrears must be dealt with first otherwise they may lose their home. They should use their savings to pay the mortgage arrears.
● They should seek advice from the bank or from a financial adviser, debt counsellor, CAB, etc.
● They need to reduce their expenditure by £1000 a month.
● The following items are regarded as non-essential and savings should be made from them immediately: savings for holiday; gym membership; clothing; magazines.
● All other items are essential and must be budgeted for.
● Car expenses may be able to reduced, depending on whether Faza needs the car.
● After all the above expenses have been reviewed, some savings could be made in, for example, food and clothing expenses.
● Faza and Ramir may be entitled to tax credit or other income support from the government.
● Ramir should try to look for another job as soon as possible.

2 Chip and PIN was introduced to try to reduce the amount of credit card/debit card fraud in the UK. It can be easy to copy someone's signature from a credit card, but if you do not know their PIN then it is more difficult to use a stolen credit card.

3 Advantages of paying by cash: paid for and owned immediately by Moyra; general advantage of only buying what you can afford/the money you have with you. Advantages of paying by credit and direct debit payment: payments are spread over 12 months, so Moyra might be able to buy a better/more expensive model than if she only had cash; the fixed monthly repayment helps with budgeting; there is no added charge for this credit and so no extra will be paid; the money will be paid direct from the bank to the shop/company and so this is convenient.

4 Alternative savings schemes: regular deposits into a savings account in the bank, building society or credit union (some accounts restrict when you can withdraw money throughout the year); saving with reputable supermarkets such as Asda and Tesco where you can save and then spend your money in the supermarket in the run-up to Christmas (such schemes should be reasonably risk-free); you could use a piggy bank to save but there is a temptation to remove money when needed, leaving less money than anticipated when Christmas arrives.

5 **a** £56.77   **b** £851.49   **c** £51.49

Quick Quiz
1 false	**2** false	**3** false	**4** true	**5** false
6 true	**7** false	**8** true	**9** false	**10** false